INVESTING

THE BILLIONAIRE'S WAY

INVESTING

THE BILLIONAIRE'S WAY

The Genius of Patience

J. RICHARD CHARLTON

Foreword by Ned Goodman

Published in 2000 by Stoddart Publishing Co. Limited
34 Lesmill Road, Toronto, Canada M3B 2T6

Distributed by:
General Distribution Services Ltd.
325 Humber College Blvd., Toronto, Canada M9W 7C3
Tel. (416) 213-1919   Fax (416) 213-1917
Email cservice@genpub.com

04 03 02 01 00   1 2 3 4 5

Canadian Cataloguing in Publication Data
available from the National Library of Canada.

ISBN 0-7737-3239-X

Cover and Text Design: Kinetics Design & Illustration

THE CANADA COUNCIL | LE CONSEIL DES ARTS
FOR THE ARTS | DU CANADA
SINCE 1957 | DEPUIS 1957

*We acknowledge for their financial support of our publishing
program the Canada Council, the Ontario Arts Council, and
the Government of Canada through the Book Publishing
Industry Development Program (BPIDP).*

Printed and bound in Canada

Contents

Foreword

BY NED GOODMAN
CHAIRMAN, PRESIDENT, AND CEO,
DUNDEE WEALTH MANAGEMENT INC.

OVER 60 years have passed since the brilliant American financial theorist Ben Graham changed the way investment professionals should look at the study and analysis of equity securities. His now time-proven policy was simple: Always require a margin of safety. His credo was even simpler: Buy shares only at prices significantly lower than their intrinsic value. His most famous protégé is Warren Buffett, who would eventually amass tens of billions of dollars as a personal fortune, and make millions of dollars for countless others who were wise enough to recognize the genius and logic behind the Graham-Buffett philosophy.

Decades after founding Berkshire Hathaway, Warren Buffett continues to use the basic disciplined approach of the Graham "security analysis" technique. He also recognizes Graham's observations about the dangerous irrationality of the millions of people who think that they are investing, but are in fact speculating — who are, indeed, "playing the market" much like one plays the horses.

Anyone who knows anything about the institution should be aware that the stock market is a complex auction mechanism that constantly swings between the extremes of under-valuation and over-valuation. (Think of a pendulum swinging back and forth in an old grandfather clock.) Unfortunately, all this occurs while most investors/speculators are fighting the powerful emotions of greed and fear.

Much has been made by later critics of Warren Buffett's eventual metamorphosis "away from" the Ben Graham style, from investing in so-called value companies to more growth-oriented firms. But to any sound investor, this growth/value distinction is illusory. The growth potential of a business is an important component of value, as much as its assets are.

The basis of Graham's philosophy is to always know the "value" of a business; when that is clear, purchase shares only when you can get a price that is discounted to that intrinsic value. To these tenets, Buffett has added several more, which he has learned from others whom he has met, read about, and worked with, along the way. The thoughts and theories of the great economist John Maynard Keynes, and those of wildly successful investors such as Philip Fisher and Charlie Munger, have allowed Buffett to fine-tune his value style of investing to the point where one can say that the style is now his invention (although he continues generously to give much of the credit to Graham).

The billionaire's investment portfolio continues to be employed in ways that are diametrically opposed to the thinking of the vast majority of stock market "players" and managers: Market forecasts are ignored, and portfolio turnovers are abhorred. Stocks are thought about as if they are the underlying business itself. And each business/stock share must be capable of being understood in fairly simple terms. A methodology such as this makes a few key demands on an investor: the mathematical probabilities of risk and reward and the willingness to use the traditional hysteria and psychology of crowds to one's own advantage.

A large number of academic studies have tried to analyse how the stock market works. And we have, in fact, come a long way towards understanding its behaviour. However, there is a big difference between understanding how it works and being able to "predict" the market.

The usually modest Buffett has admitted that he is mystified by the fact that his style of investing is still not widely accepted by academics and investment professionals. At Infinity Mutual Funds, we are proud to admit that we are going against the traditional investment crowd and inflexible academia and following Buffett's "buy-and-hold good businesses" style of investing.

Perhaps the process of knowledgeable, conscious purchases of good businesses at prices below their real value, and holding them to infinity, is too simple for academics. Obviously, the complexity of the stock market, and continual psychological concern about the risk of total loss, tends to fake out all but the most devoted followers of the billionaire's philosophy. Richard Charlton, the author of this book, has benefitted from, and is passionately devoted to, this philosophy.

An investor's personal level of risk tolerance is wound up in many various elements of behaviourial psychology. And the recent past has seen a Noah-like deluge of professional energy expended by financial planners, all devoted to attempts to assess the risk tolerances of each investor.

As Charlton is well aware, the risk tolerance of each of us is indeed complex and subject to the emotional dynamics of a changing and not always understood environment. Each one of us has a risk tolerance that is under constant siege by the events of the day.

We all know how brave and aggressive we can be in a rising market, and how meek and risk-averse we become in a falling one. Charlton, a founding shareholder of Infinity Mutual Funds, has long recognized that the "buy-and-hold good businesses" concept really does work. And it especially works in meeting the risk tolerance of every long-term investor.

In *Investing the Billionaire's Way*, Richard has written a book that allows every investor to understand, and use, the Buffett style of admittedly simplistic, but highly profitable investing. He knows that each of our individual emotions about investing is real; that we will, almost every one of us, always tend to react to those inevitable feelings of greed and fear. We will react positively to speculative, get-rich-quick ideas during ebullient times, and be very risk-averse — even against those quality businesses that we should be buying — during the bad times.

The collective market judgment is always led irrationally too far in either direction — recall that image of the grandfather clock — and no human being possesses the predictive powers that will allow him or her to be able always to act rationally during that typhoon of irrational behaviour. Over the years, Charlton has learned that the constant, inevitable gyrations of the stock markets of the world have always been unsettling to his large client base. (How could they not be?) To counter the irrationality that often accompanies that understandable discomfort, he recommends mutual funds and stocks that take advantage of the disciplined investment process of buying good businesses and holding them — through both the good and the bumpy times.

I am proud to say that the process outlined so thoughtfully and clearly in *Investing the Billionaire's Way* has been tried and proven by me, as I have had the good fortune myself to accumulate wealth by holding good businesses, both through our mutual funds and directly. Some of these I have hung onto through some very tough years, before ultimately achieving a significant payout of many times my original investment.

My company's recent purchase of the Infinity Group of Mutual Funds is testimony of my belief in the Graham-Buffett philosophy and process. It has worked so well that — to echo a popular electric shaver commercial of recent years — I bought the company. I know that you will find this book intriguing and enlightening, as Richard Charlton has filled it with that simple but profitable investment concept that has inevitably delivered superior results without undue risk. And isn't that what we all want from our investments, and for our financial future?

Some Extremely Relevant Quotations

It is a gloomy moment in the history of our country. The domestic economic situation is in chaos. Our dollar is weak throughout the world. Prices are so high as to be utterly impossible. The political cauldron seethes and bubbles with uncertainty. Russia hangs as usual, like a cloud, dark and silent, upon the horizon. It is a solemn moment. Of our troubles, no man can see the end.

The Investment Letter, *Harper's Magazine*, 1847

Thirty years ago, no one could have foreseen the huge expansion of the Vietnam war, wage and price control, two oil shocks, the resignation of a president, the dissolution of the Soviet Union, a one-day drop in the Dow of 508 points, or treasury bills fluctuating between 2.8% and 17.4%. But, surprise — none of these events made the slightest dent in Ben Graham's investment principles. Nor did they render unsound the negotiated purchases of fine businesses at sensible prices. Imagine the cost to us, then, if we had let fear of unknowns cause us to defer or alter the deployment of capital. Indeed, we have usually made our best purchases when apprehensions about some macro event were at a peak. Fear is the foe of the faddist, but the friend to the fundamentalist. A different set of major shocks is sure to occur in the next 30 years. We will neither try to predict these nor profit from them. If we can identify businesses similar to those we have purchased in the past, external surprises will have little effect on our long-term results.

WARREN BUFFETT,
the world's most successful investor,
writing nearly 150 years later

Introduction

S INCE 90% of all investment advice given out today is like a bad, even pathetic, joke ("Be sure to put money every year into your RRSP!" "Buy low and sell high!" "Invest in a house as soon as possible!" "Use asset allocation!" "Sector rotation is the way to go!"), I thought I might begin with a favourite joke of my own.

An exceedingly wealthy Canadian has decided to throw a summer party at his palatial home in Vancouver, inviting hundreds of guests into his giant backyard. As they mill about his Olympic-sized pool, the man steps forward and makes a strange announcement.

"I have decided to hold a contest tonight. As many of you have noticed, I have filled my swimming pool with giant sharks. I here offer the choice of two glorious prizes — the hand of my beautiful daughter in marriage, or one million dollars, to whoever can swim the length of the pool and survive."

1

The giant crowd gasps, and looks about at one another. True, his daughter is a wonderful catch, and a million dollars is a great offer — but what chance would any of them have to get across that shark-infested swimming pool?

The minutes tick by, and not a single person comes forward to try to claim one or the other of the fabulous prizes.

Suddenly, there is a giant *splash*, and a young man is seen in the water, swimming furiously across the pool.

After an agonizing minute or two, the fellow drags himself out of the pool on the other side, with the sharks nipping at the heels of his water-logged shoes.

"That was extraordinary!" exclaimed the host. "I truly didn't think anyone would dare to do it! Which do you want? The hand of my lovely daughter, or the one million dollars?"

The hero shakes water out of his ears and clothes and screams, "I want the sonovabitch who pushed me into the pool!"

The moral is clear. We are *all* in that pool, and for our entire lives, for it is the pool of human existence. And what are the sharks? They are inflation, taxes, bad advice. And most of all, ignorance, the ignorance nearly all of us suffer from, ignorance that prevents us from preparing ourselves financially for our retirement years. To continue the pool analogy, the sharks are the accumulated ignorance that frightens us away from reaching "the other side" we all desire so fervently: wealth, security, and happiness.

Ignorance is all around us, much like the weather. What is the difference between investing and gambling in mutual funds and stocks? Can we ever truly realize the vital importance of understanding the benefits of compound interest and capital growth? Isn't it risky to sell my GICs and Canada

Savings Bonds and invest that "secure money" in mutual funds or a portfolio of publicly traded securities? Isn't it dangerous to borrow money and risk it in any kind of investments that can fluctuate greatly?

One need not be poor or under-employed to be ignorant of these issues. I have had presidents and chairpersons of billion-dollar companies as clients who were as ignorant of the proper way to invest as anyone else; these men were capable of running giant corporations skilfully but did not know how to handle their own money.

There are doctors who can diagnose and treat diseases with the utmost skill, but when it comes to the stock market they melt away like a snowman in July. There are lawyers who can deal with the most complex court case and argue the most arcane legal points but become bumbling idiots when faced with any serious investment decision.

One of my biggest complaints about our society and our school system is that there is almost nothing that prepares us, as young boys and girls, for our financial future. Millions graduate from grade school, even high school, lacking any knowledge of the word "mortgage," much less the meaning of compound interest or the importance of borrowing to invest. (Or the foolishness of sinking hundreds of thousands of dollars into that mortgage, for that matter.) Millions enter university without knowing about Registered Retirement Savings Plans (and their innate flaws; see below). Indeed, little is taught in our schools to prepare us to manage the vast sums of money we will all earn over our respective lifetimes at our chosen occupations.

My purpose in writing this book is that I want to help countless Canadians to prepare for their retirement years —

and long before — through creating and managing wealth. Yet, perhaps surprisingly, this is not a case of being "easier said than done." I will show throughout this book that through *simple, proven laws* that have all stood the test of time, one can ignore the irrational, greedy self-destructiveness of most investors and "stock market players." (And "playing," I can assure you, is precisely what they are doing. Playing with their money and their future, which, far more often than not, they are gambling away.)

I am a firm believer that I am in the most valuable profession in the world, and one of the fastest growing: wealth management and financial planning.

What makes it so worthwhile? Well, most people make money at the expense of others: The accountant earns his living by handling another's books; the pharmacist earns her living by filling someone else's prescriptions, and so on.

I have become one of Canada's most successful investment advisors because I have managed to make hundreds upon hundreds of people wealthy. I think of one client of mine who invested some $300,000 through me several years ago. Today, his portfolio is worth over $2,000,000. This man can now retire, due to my financial advice — and how many people can say that about any other person in their lives?

My friend and mentor, Nick Murray, once put it quite bluntly: "We in the financial industry are the most valuable people in our clients' lives. We are even more important than their doctors!"

Is this extreme? Well, every doctor will ultimately lose his or her patients; they will all die. But when one helps people accumulate wealth — and that's my job, in my career and in this book — that wealth will live on for decades and transcend generations.

So, I do not personally see myself as a mutual funds salesman or as a stockbroker. Far from it. I am here to affect people's lives; to make a positive, welcome difference in their futures and the futures of their children and grandchildren.

No, you won't "get rich quick." I'll leave that for the penny-stock promoters and the people who sell lottery tickets. A handful of them will get rich, all right, but 98% will lose their wallets, if not their pants.

But if you follow the advice that I'll be sharing with you over the rest of this book, in all probability, you cannot go wrong. Better than that. You will make it successfully across that shark-infested pool of life, because no one will push you in or lead you astray. You'll be protected from all the dangers that surround you, because you will possess the precious knowledge of permanent-value investing, which is so simple a concept that it's almost embarrassing.

How simple? Read on . . .

1

From Insurance
to Mutual Funds

LIKE other readers of this book who have also taken many years to "find themselves," I did not come upon the selling of mutual funds as my first occupation; indeed, like a large percentage of present citizens of this country, Canada was not my first home, either.

I was born in Jamaica in 1950 to a mulatto father and a Sephardic-Jewish mother, which meant that I was considered a white man on that large Caribbean island. I was discriminated against in school and did not enjoy high school at all. In retrospect, I was much like so many bright but restless students who see no practical use to what they are being taught, so I dropped out of school before I was 17.

I next entered an art class, and then helped my father run some hotels in Montego Bay. I'm not sure I was much help to him, but I certainly had a wonderful time, spending endless summers in one of the great resort areas of the world.

Then, when my father sold his hotel, I went to work for him at Federal Casualty Jamaica Ltd. Insurance, a company he had founded. My dad was one of the truly great insurance men of his time, since he viewed that concept in a profound and thoughtful way. He saw insurance as not something one buys, but as a grand facility provided for the public by financial organizations whereby one could pay them to take over, and carry out, financial obligations each of us could not fulfill ourselves.

Maybe this was simply another way of selling insurance, but my father did provide for me — as I later took on a career in life insurance when I first came to Canada — an excellent basis for my knowledge; it was all that I knew about the industry.

My father proved to me that one could not use merely a purchase agreement form to buy a life insurance policy; one had to apply to an insurance company to obtain that policy. And so, throughout my brief career in the insurance world, I had phenomenal success, because Dad taught me that I was helping people to apply to these financial institutions to help them do things they couldn't do themselves — whether it was to fund a partnership, or feed their families if they did not make it safely home.

Dad also pointed out to me that one of the most certain, honourable things in financial planning is adequate life insurance — by setting up a financial contract to allow the insurance company to take over those responsibilities one might not, one day, be able to handle on one's own.

He dramatized for me how much debt a young family man is forced to undertake in this society, whether for a car, a house, or furniture. He showed me how, when a person dies, the banks and trust companies have no problem with repossessing it all, if those debts are not paid off.

Ah, but they will never repossess your wife and children, he would say. That was one answer he gave when he frequently heard the shocking declaration, "Why should I buy life insurance? When I die, that's their problem." I used to wonder how anyone with a spouse and kids could say something like that; it simply blew me away.

My father had an even better response: "The Lord might provide, all right, but that provision might be a dingy tenement for your family to live in, and a washtub for your wife to sweat over. If you truly love your family, one of the cornerstones of life should be to pay an insurance company to take care of this responsibility for you."

Dad brought many new types of insurance to the island of Jamaica: casualty, health, and accident insurance (for cancer and other sicknesses, as well as accidents); manslaughter policies (since in that country, the car, not the driver, is insured, so every driver had to have insurance for both court costs and his defence). So when I emigrated to Canada in 1973, I was well prepared to make a career in the insurance business, since I believed profoundly in the concept.

I Turn against My Beloved Profession

I soon had an excellent career, selling insurance and helping people to apply for life insurance, at Mutual Life of Canada, from 1974 to 1976. From the casualty insurance I had sold with my father back in Jamaica, I now entered the life insurance business, and I became a passionate promoter of the service.

But I also grew antagonistic and even hostile to insurance companies that sold Registered Retirement Savings Plans (RRSPs), which were, in effect, registered whole life insurance policies — but the individual had zero cash value for seven years. And the salesman? He had the good fortune of being paid 130% of the premium/RRSP contribution in the first year.

I soon realized that there is truly no such thing as life insurance. After all, we will all die, one day. Life insurance is simply something to fund that eventuality. Insurance companies will use mortality tables to figure out how long someone will "be here"; they will use interest rate assumptions to set up the sinking fund, and also purchase reinsurance to share the risk of what happens if you get knocked down while crossing the street.

But if you don't get hit by that truck, you'll be here a long time. And that ends up being a very long time to pay premiums into a sinking fund, where insurance companies for years have used an assumption of low interest rates — for example, 2% — while turning right around and actually loaning those premiums out at 8% in mortgages. Not a bad deal — for them. (In Toronto, one can see all the tall, well-appointed, fully-paid-for buildings up and down University Avenue.)

I slowly grew to recognize that insurance companies are phenomenally rich organizations precisely because they have consistently used the ignorance of most individuals to fill their own coffers, and make the people who own those companies very, very wealthy.

How wealthy? Well, the common stocks of insurance companies listed on the exchanges of the world are among the greatest businesses in the world. As I shall note several times in this book, the wildly successful Berkshire Hathaway holding company out of Omaha, Nebraska, is deeply engaged in the insurance business, because while those insurance firms are waiting those long years to pay the inevitable liability for one's injury or death they have the use of the money. Several of the billions that Warren Buffett has so brilliantly invested in Coca-Cola, Gillette, and other internationally renowned businesses have come from the profits of the giant insurance companies he owns. (Canadians are said to be "over-insured," but they are really over-premiumed and underinsured.)

What Drove Me Crazy about the Insurance Industry

One scenario really bothered me about the industry I worked for with such passion and such determination, and it's a classic argument: Holders of life insurance can borrow against the "cash surrender value" of their policy, and use those proceeds as they wish.

Hardly. "Rip-off" is the best description I can use for this. Let me explain. If someone has, say, a $10,000 policy with $3000 of cash value, one can borrow one's own sinking fund (by this I mean that the cash surrender value, which is the reserve, or sinking fund). So far, so good.

So, you borrow that money, while continually paying the premium on that $10,000 policy, along with the interest for that $3000 loan. Fair enough. But then you drop dead, and what does the insurance company do? It will pay your beneficiaries only $7000, because that $3000 is considered an advance on the death benefit.

Things like that began to annoy me more and more. (I should mention that Canada has come a long way since I was in the insurance business, over two decades ago, and it's only fair to note that the pushing of this type of insurance, certainly since the late 1980s, has subsided to a great degree.)

So the insurance companies back then, and their many agents, would insist that "whole life policies" were the better deal. They weren't, of course. The bottom line is, people should insist that their insurance be pure insurance, by which I mean either term or straight insurance. There is simply no need whatsoever, in my opinion, for people to have any form of insurance with cash surrender value associated with it. Permanent or renewable term is more than sufficient, and a far better deal. (The idea, when I was in the industry, was that each person just *had* to have "whole life," because you wanted to be able to convert it to term in your later years. But today there actually is permanent term, which goes straight up to the age of 100, so why blow all that money on the vastly more costly whole life, which comes with that utterly unnecessary "cash surrender value" built in?)

Naturally, some kind of life insurance is vitally important for estate planning purposes, and since I am always talking about creating "multi-generational wealth" with my clients I cannot ignore the concept. The question is, what kind of life insurance will best allow their great-grandchildren to manage the wealth of their grandchildren, which I originally helped to create for them?

As I shall note frequently throughout this book, Revenue Canada is our partner. And on the death of the final spouse of a family, that institution deems that there is a disposition that took place to all of one's heirs. So I believe it is essential to apply for life insurance on the joint lives of both husband and wife. This pays a tax-free lump sum to the last to die, whereas the premiums will stop at the death of the first spouse. Then, tax-free amounts of money are deposited to the estate, which creates liquidity. I suggest this on a continual basis, to avoid selfish management fees, and consider it an important part of estate and financial planning.

I Make the Leap from Insurance to Mutual Funds

What finally broke this camel's back was a classic ploy of the insurance industry two decades ago. They kept licensing an endless number of agents who kept bombing out of the business every month. So there was this continuous stream of new people coming in, putting new policies onto the books, and then soon leaving the business.

The insurance companies were constantly saying (if not in so many words), "Hey, all of you new agents. Give me the names of your friends and relatives, and I'll sell them insurance." But in order to leverage their constantly shifting human resources, they would be proclaiming this to many thousands of new agents. Of course, after each of those new agents left the insurance industry, they also left something else: their friends and relatives to pay those (invariably too-high) premiums indefinitely.

That is really what the insurance industry was all about back then.

I remember going to see my closest friends and relatives to sell them insurance. One person I called upon was Phil

Shearn. He and his wife Rose were friends from Jamaica, and I eagerly visited them with my branch manager at Mutual Life, Jack O'Neill, back in 1974.

We sold Phil a retirement savings plan: It was a Mutual Life of Canada policy called "R25 at 65." The plan meant that every $2500 you deposited came due when you — the client — reached the age of 65. It was, quite literally, an endowment policy that would endow, at one's retirement age, exactly what the person put into it — with little or no interest whatsoever.

Not everyone lost from this deal, of course. It paid me over 100% of the first year's premium or the RRSP contribution, over $4000. I was thrilled.

But I really had no idea what I was doing for my clients — or to them. When Phil read the contract carefully, he quickly exercised his "recision rights," which essentially meant "I want my money back."

When he explained to me what I had done to him, I was flooded with both shame and embarrassment. God knows, I was utterly mortified at my actions. It was a disgusting contract of insurance, sold under the guise of an RRSP. I was mortified, all right — and furious. And so I decided to launch a crusade against the insurance industry.

The first thing I did was urge every client I had to purchase only (inexpensive and sufficient) term insurance, and to invest the cash surrender value into something worthwhile. (The rest of this book will be dedicated to showing you what is truly "worthwhile" investing in.)

I also helped to introduce new life insurance policies that carried a single premium that assumed a higher rate of interest. And so I was soon visiting some of Hamilton, Ontario's most prominent businessmen and offering to replace their insurance — to double the face amount of the insurance for the cash surrender value in their current policies, and totally wipe out any future premiums.

Around this time, a friend of mine named James Bullock wrote a series of articles entitled "Life Insurance: The Myth and the Mystery" for the now-defunct business newspaper, *The Financial Times of Canada*. His writings were so critical of that industry, I actually had fantasies that Jimmy and I might be assassinated by friends of the insurance companies because of our actions.

People like me were hardly alone in our "war" against the dubious workings of the insurance industry back in the 1970s, nor were these struggles limited to Canada alone. While I was personally replacing, on behalf of my clients, more whole life insurance policies with term insurance than you could imagine, there was a real uprising in the United States as well.

Indeed, a huge industry grew in reaction to the then-dubious machinations of the insurance companies, such as the A.L. Williams Group, which soon became one of the United States' largest and most successful groups and it quickly came to Canada. The story behind that company's origins was not dissimilar to the experiences of my friend Phil, who discovered how unfair his coverage was and raised my consciousness at the same time.

The father of Mr. Williams was over-premiumed and under-insured, and when the man died prematurely his mother collected very little in the way of benefits — after all those years that her husband was paying huge sums of money. Unlike me, that family not only went to war against traditional insurance practices, but actually created a mass movement across North America to "buy term and invest the difference."

Around this time, I met a remarkable individual and fellow Jamaican whom I consider one of my mentors and best friends to this day: Michael Lee-Chin. He was, and is, one of the most powerful people I've ever met, because of his amazing ability to implement what other people might consider "just a good idea."

I first met Mike in 1976 when he was working for Investors Group, one of Canada's major mutual funds companies. I had recently left Mutual Life of Canada and had formed an independent brokerage agency called Quantum. He actually sought me out, and for a rather humorous reason: He had heard about "another very successful Jamaican fellow who also drives a Mercedes-Benz in Hamilton, Ontario."

He wanted to recruit me to join him. He was unsuccessful at first, but we quickly formed an acquaintanceship and ultimately a friendship, as I spoke of my belief that most life insurance companies were exploiting people out of their ignorance. He, in turn, talked about the investment business through his then-still-captive eyes of a representative at Investors — which only sells its own mutual funds.

By late 1978, Mike left Investors to open a branch office for Regal Capital Planners, and successfully recruited me to join him. And so I finally became involved in the investment business. He would describe to me how well people who invested $10,000 in certain mutual funds did, compared with those who invested in various bank offerings, such as Guaranteed Income Certificates (GICs), and I was overwhelmed. I was shaken by the concept of mutual funds and how they worked.

It is fortunate that I had introduced Michael Lee-Chin to life insurance — the term kind, of course — because it would be life insurance sales that helped the two of us through the lean years of the 1981-84 recession, when high interest rates discouraged the purchase of mutual funds. During that rough time, we also concentrated on estate planning.

Then, when the stock market rebounded healthily in 1984, Michael came to me in the wee hours — it may have been 1 a.m. — and exclaimed, "Richard, why not go and see your best insurance clients and tell them, 'If you don't believe that now is a fantastic time to invest, just give me $2000, and I'll put it into four different mutual funds for you. We'll see what happens.' "

It was in this fashion that I built some of my most successful and faithful clients, who are with me to this day. In fact, there are several clients for whom I still keep that original $2000 invested "on the books," just to remind them of the importance of being patient, long-term investors.

The importance of patience? More like the genius of patience. Each $500 that I invested in mutuals such as Trimark Fund and Mackenzie Industrial American is now worth well over $5000. What better proof could one have for my successful, reliable, yet simple theory — and the subject of this book — of "buy quality investments and hold them long term"?

And I Move On, in a Zigzag Course, to AIC Funds

Throughout the mid-1980s, Michael Lee-Chin and I sold mutual funds for Regal Capital Planners, which was then — and is still now — run by the admirable and wise Paul Rockel. He is a lovely man, and a true visionary in the mutual funds industry. He had a dramatic impact on me, as did Michael, as they both explained to me the value of mutual funds and professional management. I would not leave Regal until 1985.

Back then, I knew very little about the actual companies that handled and managed the mutual funds, nor was I at all aware of the concept of investing in publicly traded securities on the stock markets of North America; I was simply a mutual funds salesman. I did a brief sojourn at Stuart Mutuals, and then finally, in the fall of 1987, joined my old friend Michael at Advantage Investment Counsel, aka AIC.

My first position was as branch manager of their Oakville office, and what I learned there is central to many of the themes and philosophies expressed throughout this book. AIC had been a poorly performing group of mutual funds that Michael Lee-Chin had purchased from an existing mutual fund company a few years earlier. And from 1985 to 1987, the managers of those so-so funds — which were nothing but a hodgepodge of equities — had no real focus or philosophy.

Then, the moment of truth. Michael decided to fire all those managers who had "come with the funds" he had purchased, and the two of us decided that we certainly could not do any worse than if we chose to implement the investment principles of Warren Buffett.

How right we were. It was at that moment, back in 1987, when the AIC funds really started to take off, in both reputation and success.

I assisted Michael as his senior vice president of marketing, not only in building a sales force but in helping our salespeople to become passionately committed to our principles. I used a two-pronged approach: to build assets in mutual funds, and to help the Canadian public to invest, rather than speculate, in publicly traded securities.

During those first, struggling years of the late 1980s, I would call on many brokerage firms and open the door for future marketing opportunities for our own AIC marketing department, and I formed liaisons with major firms to promote our funds. The ones responsible for their invariably wise and inspired purchases — more on this below — were Michael Lee-Chin, of course, and Jonathan Wellum. I knew every stock they chose, and had personal, in-depth knowledge of every business we invested in, because they were all discussed extensively with me. But I never picked any of them myself, as I never saw myself as a money manager. I am a theorist and a portfolio strategist rather than a portfolio analyst.

Not that I had to pick them! Michael Lee-Chin was and is a brilliant strategist and implementer, who would grab an idea and run with it; only then would he fine-tune it. "Ready, fire, *aim!*" is the way I describe it. And in his hands, this kind of activity rarely failed. Highly motivated and caring, Michael, Jonathan, and I were all profoundly committed to the magnificent principles of Warren Buffett, which I will discuss in depth in the pages to come.

In brief, we believed that stocks are parts of businesses

and not merely pieces of paper that one trades back and forth, like baseball cards. That's not a business or investing; that's guesswork and gambling. Investors who sector-rotate and asset allocate and market-time are simply gamblers, not true investors. The only true investor is one who does what the variety store owner does: He buys a business, goes to work every day, and earns money, slowly but surely. That's investing. And that was the difference between the philosophy of AIC funds and every other mutual fund manager who calls himself a "money manager." (Since I became a founding shareholder in 1997 of a new family of mutual funds, Infinity, based on time-tested principles of a sound investment philosophy, I can now include myself in this same select group.)

Now, what do I mean by a sound investment philosophy? You're about to see.

2

A Recipe for Life
and Investing

WE all need role models in our lives. In many cases, it's our mother or our father; sometimes it's a world leader, such as a Gandhi or a Martin Luther King; other times, it's a poet, a scientist, a sports figure, even a movie star. My recipe for success in life is quite straightforward:

- Identify a role model for yourself.
- Find his or her "recipe" for success and copy it exactly.
- Implement it.

As you can see, there is no reinventing of the wheel going on here. Since I used the word "recipe," let me continue the metaphor. Imagine you are at a friend's home for dinner, and you are served a delicious bread pudding for dessert. You like it so much, you just have to have the recipe.

Provided you are given the exact measurements — the

correct amount of milk, bread, and raisins (and not "a pinch of this and a dash of that") — you could make the same bread pudding as our friend, because you had the recipe.

Well, imagine if you could get your hands on the recipe for successful investing. Before I give you the recipe, let me introduce you to the master chef — and certainly my own, personal role model in my life as an investor — Warren Buffett. He is the richest and smartest businessman and investor in the United States, with a net worth in excess of $30 billion (and counting!) as of the fall of 1999.

In 1956, Mr. Buffett collected $105,100 from family and friends in Omaha, Nebraska, plus $100 from his own pocket, and started the Buffett Limited Partnership. This was an investment company in which he, as manager, received 25% of profit after investors received a 6% return on capital.

The fund prospered tremendously. Over its 13-year lifetime, the original investment compounded at 29.5% annually to reach about $100 million.

But by 1969, the market was so speculative and stock prices so high, that Mr. Buffett could no longer find any companies that met his strict criteria for investing. So he folded the partnership, gave back most of the money to the shareholders, along with a proportional interest in a textile company called Berkshire Hathaway Inc., which he acquired in 1965.

The textile company, plagued by a history of financial troubles, finally closed. The new Berkshire Hathaway became a holding company, owning significant stakes in companies such as GEICO Corp., Gillette Co., Coca-Cola Co., Washington Post Co., Wells Fargo & Co., General Dynamics Corp., and Salomon Brothers Inc.

If you had put $10,000 in the original Buffett Limited Partnership, then converted to Berkshire Hathaway in 1965, your money would be worth over $250 million in late 1999. This is, quite simply, the most successful investment of all time.

As you can see, Mr. Buffett is not only an investor but also a businessman, which brings me to the recipe. He believes in buying good businesses at good prices and staying with them as long as they remain good — and never selling, regardless of how high the stock price gets. "What would be the point?" he asks. "You might invest the money in something less great!"

He does not try to time the stock markets or catch swings. "Don't try and figure out what the market is doing," he has said. "Figure out businesses you understand, and concentrate. Diversification is protection against ignorance, but if you don't feel ignorant, the need for it goes down drastically."

Mr. Buffett's Rip Van Winkle–style of investing reflects his view that the stock market serves to move assets from the active to the patient. He says he knows of no individual or institution that has been successful at timing the market — "flitting from flower to flower," as he describes it. You will eventually sell your flowers to water your weeds.

Mr. Buffett does not buy stocks. Stocks are an abstraction. He buys businesses, or parts of businesses if the whole thing is not for sale. As he has said, "What I like is economic strength in an area I understand and where I think it will last. For example, it is very difficult to think of two companies in the world in important areas that have the presence of Coke and Gillette, two of Berkshire Hathaway's core holdings."

One of the most important times to reflect on the Buffett

recipe and to be comforted by it is during severe stock market corrections or prolonged bear market periods. It is in those times that you will be forced to examine the inherent value in your stocks or mutual funds.

If your investment decisions were not based on a judgment about short-term prospects for the stock market, but rather reflected an opinion about long-term business prospects for specific companies, you would be less inclined to be upset and be scared out of your stocks at the wrong time.

Stock market corrections, just like the changing seasons, are a normal occurrence. As with the weather, if you know that corrections are inevitable, then you will be mentally prepared to be patient during them. You will hibernate with your stocks and mutual funds during the long winter, knowing that in the spring new growth will return.

As corporate earnings improve and stock markets head higher, articles of doom are appearing frequently in Canada and the United States, showing little sign of abating. The stock market is truly climbing a "wall of worry." These articles are a distracting annoyance because they are targeted at people's fear, which is destructive to their long-term investment objectives. It is interesting to note that as recently as 1990-91, there were no articles forecasting the current buoyant markets. It seems some journalists take pleasure in trying to scare investors out of their mutual funds and stocks.

Several years ago, Mr. Buffett said in his annual report that if you're in a poker game and you don't know in the first half-hour who the patsy is, you're the patsy.

How does this apply to investing?

If the stock market goes down 10% and you want to buy more because the business is worth just as much, then the stock market is the patsy.

So, while anything can happen in stock markets, this does not have to concern the investor. The market crash of 1987 was probably an aberration caused by excessive computer program trading. Silly instruments cause silly prices. Astute investors can take advantage of these prices or ignore them.

The recipe for investing from the most successful investor of all time seems almost too simple. But then again, most things are.

What's So Special about
Mr. Buffett's Holding Company?

Berkshire Hathaway Inc. owns subsidiaries in a good number of diverse business activities. The most important of these is the property and casualty insurance business, conducted on both a direct and reinsurance basis through a number of subsidiaries, collectively referred to as the Berkshire Hathaway Insurance Group.

Investment portfolios of insurance subsidiaries include meaningful equity ownership percentages of other publicly traded companies. At the end of 1999, these investments included 100% of the capital stock of GEICO Corporation, of which Berkshire Hathaway owned but 48% just five years earlier; over 50 million shares of the Walt Disney Company and another 50 million of American Express; nearly 100 million shares off the Gillette Company; over 200 million shares of the Coca-Cola Company; approximately 15% of the

Washington Post Company (which includes *Newsweek* magazine); approximately 12% of the common stock of Wells Fargo & Company; approximately 14% of the common stock of General Dynamics Corporation and common and convertible preferred stock of Salomon Inc., which have around 15% of the total voting power of that company. And in late December 1998, Berkshire Hathaway completed a $22-billion acquisition of General Re Corp, which is the largest U.S. property-casualty reinsurer, and which owns 82% of the oldest reinsurance company in the world, Cologne Re. Together, the two firms reinsure all lines of insurance and operate in 124 countries. Not bad.

If all that isn't diverse enough for you, Berkshire Hathaway also publishes the *Buffalo News*, a daily and Sunday newspaper in western New York. Other business activities conducted by non-insurance subsidiaries include publication and distribution of encyclopedias and related educational and instructional material (World Book and Childcraft products); manufacture and marketing of home cleaning systems and related accessories (sold principally under the Kirby name); manufacture and sale of boxed chocolates and other confectionary products (See's Candies), retailing of home furnishings (Nebraska Furniture Mart); manufacture and distribution of uniforms (Fechheimer Brothers Company); manufacture, import, and distribution of footwear (H.H. Brown Shoe Company, Lowell Shoe, Inc. and Dexter Shoe Company); and the manufacture and distribution of air compressors, air tools, and painting systems (Campbell Hausfeld products).

There are several other businesses owned by Mr. Buffett's Berkshire Hathaway, each engaged in a variety of other —

invariably successful — activities. All of them are seemingly "ordinary" businesses that produce extraordinary returns.

Once again, Warren Buffett's track record has been nothing less than phenomenal. It is interesting and informative that Berkshire Hathaway is the single most highly priced security listed on any exchange in any country in the world. As I write these words in the dying weeks of 1999, a single share on the New York Stock Exchange is worth nearly $60,000. Yet in the summer of 1997, when an earlier version of this book went to press, the price was "only" $47,700! Four years earlier, one could snap up that same share for little over $20,000. And just a few years before that, for around $6000. And that was before Berkshire Hathaway had purchased either GEICO or General Re, both multi-billion-dollar companies.

If you were not familiar with either Mr. Buffett or his astonishing holding company, you might have been taken aback a little by the variety of the businesses: car insurance? soft drinks? razor blades? newspapers? home cleaning systems? encyclopedias? chocolates? shoes? furniture? What on earth could they all have in common?

(Do you recall the excellent point made in that best-selling business book of the 1980s *In Search of Excellence*? "Stick to your knitting," the authors warned all potential business people. If you are in computers, don't sell detergents on the side. And look what happened when Gerber's, the baby food people, started to expand into other, unrelated fields. They lost millions upon millions of dollars.)

But there is something critically and profoundly similar about all the businesses owned (or partly owned) by Mr. Buffett's company: They are all — every single one of them

— superior businesses with strong economic fundamentals. They are all businesses that were purchased at good, fair prices and that have never been sold, as long as they have remained good businesses.

Remember what I said, earlier in this chapter. To Warren Buffett — and to me, since he is my mentor — the stock market is utterly and totally irrelevant (I'll have more to say about that later). The only purpose it really serves is as a reference, to see who is offering to do something stupid — or something smart.

Far too many of us — probably the vast majority of us — need immediate gratification from the stock market's daily listings ("Look! ABC Inc. went up 2 points!" "Oh, no! My shares of XYZ Ltd. have fallen ¼! What am I to do?") in order to validate our well-being, our sense of emotional, if not financial, self-worth.

The only thing that matters to my mentor, Warren Buffett — and to me, his disciple — is the quality of the businesses owned. Mr. Buffett sees the stock market, in the short term, as a voting machine that requires a voter registration test based only on money, and not on emotional stability or on intelligence. In the long run, it is a weighing machine. But if the quality of the businesses one buys are good, with strong earnings, then eventually one will have higher stock prices. (And note that I write "eventually"; those higher stock prices do not necessarily come overnight, or in the next few weeks.)

What has that philosophy done for Mr. Warren Buffett of Omaha? It has given him a net worth of over $30 billion, as of late 1999. (That net worth was only around $9.5 billion five years earlier. Have you tripled your net worth in the past half-decade?)

Ah, you may say, "This Buffett guy is pretty impressive, but what about risk? I'm terrified to risk my money — and the money my wife, my children, and I will need in the future — on something as insecure as the stock market or mutual funds. What should I do?"

Several things. Such as reading the next chapter.

3

Let's Define "Risk"

I BELIEVE that we are presently on the verge of an epidemic crisis of monolithic proportions. A huge army of men and women, known as Baby Boomers — those born between 1946 and 1964 and numbering close to 80 million in the United States alone — will be marching into and through middle age and old age over the next three or four decades. (The latest demographics tell us that, every eight minutes, another person turns 50.) The vast majority of those people will be unprepared and undercapitalized, because they did not understand "risk," and how inflation will erode the purchasing ability of their capital.

We must, therefore, learn to properly define "risk." I define that word in two ways, qualitatively and quantitatively. In other words, how much risk is there, and what is the quality of that risk?

Consider a woman who invests in a powerful business

like Atlanta-based Coca-Cola, and a man who chooses to drive to Niagara Falls, Ontario, for the weekend, and play the roulette wheel or try his skill at the casino's blackjack table.

Both are taking risks. But surely we can determine that even though both activities involve risk, the quality and the quantity of each are vastly different.

The real problem with the way most of us view risk is that we learned our definition of risk (and safety) from our parents, who in turn learned it from their parents. And the latter were, by and large, children of the Great Depression — those long, hungry, insecure, and terrifying years of the 1930s.

Peter Lynch, in his best-seller *Beating the Street*, notes that the stock market crash of 1929 and the Depression that followed are both responsible for having kept two generations of potential investors away from share ownership, yet it has been inflation and taxes that have done more damage to erode capital than a dozen stock market crashes could ever have accomplished.

In 1893, just three generations ago, the life expectancy of the average individual in North America was a mere 33 years; just over one century later, that expectancy is well over 70 for men, close to 80 for women. This has led to great changes in our attitudes towards our health. Today, a person dreading the winter and entering the flu season might say to himself, "I'd better not catch the flu; I might have to take a week off work." Yet only one generation ago, he might have declared, "I hope I don't get the flu, because I might die."

As the 20th century came to a close, a man or woman who made it to 60 stood a good chance of living well into his or her 90s. The man will live a decade or two longer than his father, while his wife could well live a full decade longer than her now-longer-lasting spouse.

In my opinion, the traditional financial services industry has (tragically) done a good job of discrediting patient, long-term investing in the shares of great businesses — the Warren Buffett way — and instead promises results from speculative and aggressive trading practices that generate commissions on every transaction. The only people who made money by these all-too-common actions were the brokers, not the clients. It was as if pharmacists kept pushing you to purchase drugs you didn't need (thus earning fees from each prescription), or doctors who run medical labs insisting on frequent but unnecessary tests that were a total waste of time for all involved but drummed up great business for their technicians.

Nothing on the face of this earth can provide you with the capital appreciation that owning shares of the world's great businesses will give you. Furthermore, history has shown that by owning those shares of quality companies, you never have to take spectacular actions (or even the slightest risks) to achieve spectacular results.

A single, quite striking example. There has never been a time in the past eight decades that you, your parents, or your grandparents should *not* have been permanent shareholders of Coca-Cola.

In 1919, Coke went public at $40 a share. In 1993, those shares, held for nearly 70 years with all dividends reinvested, were worth over $2.2 million each. (As of late 1999, that number was actually over $5 million — more than double again, in little over half a decade.)

But let's not go back that far. In 1938, when most of our

parents had at least a few dollars to "risk," a fresh $40 then invested in Coca-Cola would be worth $25,000 by the end of 1993, and many thousands more, by the end of the century. Between 1983 and 1993, Coca-Cola ranked number 72 out of the top 100 performing businesses listed on the New York Stock Exchange, with an astounding return of over 1200%. In fact, $100,000 invested in 1983 was worth over $1.2 million only a decade later, and more than double that amount by late 1999.

Even shorter term, when Warren Buffett of Berkshire Hathaway chose to invest a further $1.23 billion into Coca-Cola in the spring of 1989, the value of these shares of Coke increased to nearly $5 billion five years later, and well over $10 billion today. This is what happens when a company — a great, powerful company like Coca-Cola — produces an annualized total return (stock appreciation plus dividends) of approximately 28%, between 1981 and the end of 1996. And even with the disappointing 1999 year for Coke (during which time the company took control of such major brands as Canada Dry, Dr. Pepper, and Schweppes from London, England–based Cadbury), 10 of 21 analysts surveyed by *Bloomberg News* maintained a "buy" recommendation for Coke shares, with eight more recommending a neutral "hold." Not too shabby for a stock that bounced between $47 and $75 over that difficult 12-month period — one of its few "losing" times in its glorious history.

What Battle Are We Fighting Here?

Some believe that the battle is knowledge versus ignorance. In many cases, it is. But as in the case of so much of investing, the *real* battle is fear versus faith.

Twenty years ago, if someone sat in his broker's office and exclaimed, "No, I do not want to own a portfolio of the world's greatest businesses," he was termed "a risk-averse investor." This is an oxymoron, like "live recording" or "military intelligence." That foolish individual was not an investor, nor was he "risk averse." He was a saver.

Most of us have been taught, whether by teachers or by parents — all of whom suffered through the Great Depression either directly or through their respective families' horror stories of riding the rails, selling apples on street corners, or lining up in ubiquitous soup kitchens — that "saving is a wise and intelligent thing to do."

I disagree. A saver is someone who looks back into the past with fear. He does not want to own anything, and only hopes to lend his money short-term, and for a guarantee (read "Guaranteed Investment Certificate"; read "Canada Savings Bond"), because he is always expecting the next Armageddon, the next Crash, the next Depression.

That's not the way the wise investor acts. He or she looks forward into the future with faith, and believes in the possibilities of and recognizes the benefits of owning businesses — or shares of them, which can be just as worthwhile.

Indeed, our poor investor was not really "risk averse," he was "loss averse." He did not understand the essential difference between temporary fluctuations in the value of shares of great businesses and the loss of principal.

What it all comes down to is this: Canadians and Americans are notoriously bad investors who are self-destructive when managing their personal portfolios. They get most of their information from the news media (which I like to call the Antichrist of investing), while neglecting professional advice from dedicated individuals.

What they do instead is pathetic: They rely upon the no-load (or the "no-help," as I like to call it) mutual fund industry. These bad advice people, as I like to call them, also include the banks, which are recent players in the world of mutual funds. So, when "GIC refugees" asked their bank teller, in 1994, to put them into "the fund that pays 40% a year," they were sold bond funds that promptly declined in value as interest rates rose. It was a case of inexperienced people advising inexperienced people who did not wish to invest in mutual funds in the first place.

Is there a risk in the world of equities? I believe that the greatest risk — the most dangerous risk, indeed the mother of all risks — in equities is in not owning them at all. And people who allow themselves to be distracted by the apocalypse du jour will live to regret it. What's interesting about the current apocalypse is that it's much like the cross-town bus: If you miss one of them, you can be sure another will come along in a few minutes.

The real risk in not investing is not the risk of principal loss. No, that's simply a minor risk. The *real* risk of not investing is the continuous erosion of your capital while you are alive.

The best example of this tragic condition is only a few feet away from where you are now sitting, at least if you are like me. Look into your pantry, and note the price of the can of beans way in the back: 29 cents? 39 cents? And the price of the can that you recently bought "on sale" — 79 cents.

Or look through some of the old letters you have saved from loved ones, mailed to you years ago. That 10-cent U.S. stamp would get a letter across the breadth of the United States in 1974. Ten years later, it would take a 20-cent U.S. stamp to get the same service. Today, the cost has more than tripled, to 33 cents, to mail a letter across the United States.

In Canada, in 1974, a stamp cost 8 cents. Just a quarter century later, the cost is nearly 50 cents, when one includes the Goods and Services Tax (GST). Over six times the cost, in less than a quarter century, to mail the same letter in Canada. These are but a few common, yet quite dramatic, examples of inflation in North America.

We often pride ourselves on how low the inflation rate is, in Canada and the United States, and with good reason: Runaway inflation in Germany, Argentina, and many Middle Eastern countries since the 1920s has often been nightmarish, with clerks changing prices hourly on articles of clothing and produce. Still, those dust-covered cans of beans in the back of our pantries, and those envelopes lovingly saved in our closets with those "cheap" stamps on their upper right-hand corners, should give us pause, even in this country, and even over the past few decades.

It is vital that we learn to ignore the worries of the world long enough to allow our investments in the great businesses of our times to be successful. On July 8, 1932, the Dow Jones Industrials recorded an intra-day low of 40.56. On January 31, 1994, the same Dow Jones recorded an intra-day high of 4000. (Need I even mention the level of 6000, reached in the early fall of 1996, barely two and a half years later, 6500, just a few short weeks after that, and 7000 in early 1997? And over 9000 in April 1998? And over 10,000 in late March 1999?) In less than seven decades, more wealth was created for the shareholders of North American businesses than at any other period in the history of the world, and more than any other asset class in existence.

Ignore the Market

The key to success in investing is to ignore the market and its so-called "risks" and patiently hold strong "earning machines" known as businesses — and for the long haul.

As of late 1999, as I write these words, inflation is lower than it has been in years, but it is always present, always ready to eat up savings and increase prices. There is a dragon in all of our lives, and it consists of inflation and rising costs, pushing us towards the agonizing dilemma of outliving our capital. But there is a St. George, too, to help slay that killer dragon: the ownership of great businesses, like the ones which Warren Buffett has purchased for his Berkshire Hathaway holding company, businesses that are always finding new and exciting ways of making money for their shareholders.

Barely over a decade ago, we all experienced — through radio, TV, and newspapers — the most significant world event since Christopher Columbus happened upon the New World: the fall of communism and the tearing down of the Berlin Wall. This was not only a political victory, of course. It was an economic victory for the people, who are the true, practising capitalists of the world. In the first hours after the wall was torn down, millions of men and women crossed over into freedom, just to see what it felt like to walk into West Germany without being shot. Three questions were heard, over and over again, as the most asked that fateful night. They were "Where is McDonald's?" "Where can I buy Levi's?" "Where can I buy a Coke?"

Echoing these extraordinary phrases, in terms of the stunningly powerful impact of great companies with universally recognized brand names, is a line recently expressed by Warren Buffett: "It is very comforting to go to bed at night knowing that over 2.5 billion males will get up in the morning and shave with Gillette."

As I noted at the start of this chapter, we are on the cusp of a global capitalist revolution. Never before in history have the world's great businesses been given true access to over six billion people around the globe — many of whom would love to have their own phone, their own car — or simply to purchase a hamburger and a glass of Coke, while sitting in their Levi jeans.

And to think that many people wonder why Warren Buffett has put such faith in such "simple" things as soft drinks, razor blades, newspapers, shoes, and furniture. It's because he doesn't believe in risk. Or in fear. Or in "saving."

Only through true investing — intelligent, long-term investing in quality businesses — will our futures be assured, and the inevitable risks of inflation and rising costs be defeated and vanquished.

4

Getting Ready for the
Five Laws of Wealth Creation

IN the last chapter, I only hinted at the quite frightening picture that will speak to a large percentage of North Americans when they turn 65 or 70: the prospect of poverty, of despair, of diminishing lifestyle, even of hunger. (Or maybe you expect the federal and provincial governments to actually continue the pensions and social insurance we've counted on for so many decades? And even if they do, do you honestly believe it will be "enough" for you and your spouse to live on?)

In early November 1996, my worst fear came walking into my office. Mr. and Mrs. Johnson (I'll call them), aged 86 and 80. They were brought to me by a friend, who somehow expected me to work a miracle for them.

And a miracle was what they needed. This couple had been retired for 26 years, and had just about exhausted the principal of their savings, because they had never invested.

"Why on earth didn't the two of you invest?" I asked them.

"Because we were afraid of losing our money," was their reply.

They did not invest, because they feared poverty. But by not investing, they had brought about the very thing they most feared. These two elderly people had come to my office with only $35,000 to their names, and expected me to turn it into an adequate income investment to support them for the rest of their lives. I didn't like their chances, but I tried my best for them.

The Johnsons should have been investing over the course of their long lives, but instead they made a commitment to buy those always-safe, always-reliable (and always disappointing) GICs, and those GICs let them down terribly. This would be a good place to quote from a powerful letter to the editor of the *Globe and Mail*'s Report on Business section, published on October 21, 1996. Sadly, it came out too late to help that pathetic elderly couple in my office, who came to me only a few weeks later. Written by a Tom Connolly of Cobourg, Ontario, it was responding to an earlier letter that had expressed "shock" that three York University professors had suggested that "retirees would be better off with more equities." I quote from the letter:

> To fund retirement, one should consider dividend income, not gains from trading. A retiree should buy and hold good-quality common stocks.
>
> For instance, if an investor had purchased Bank of Nova Scotia common stock in the fall of 1990 when it was trading at $11.12, the investor would now be receiving a dividend of $1.36 a share or 12% on the investment.

After factoring in the benefit of the Canadian dividend tax credit, the yield is in the order of 16%. I can easily fund my retirement lifestyle with a yield of 16%. Furthermore, this 16% does not include gains on the stock price, and next year the dividend will go up again.

Alternatively, in the fall of 1990, an investor could have opted for a five-year guaranteed investment certificate paying 11.25%. Last fall, the GIC would have had to be renewed at 6.5% — a decrease in income of 42.7%. [Note from the author: by the fall of 1996, you could not get a GIC paying more than 2½% — for a stunning *decrease* of income of *well over 80%*.]

Common stocks can provide an increasing income so that retirees do not have to spend capital. The income from a bond is fixed and cheapens with inflation.

It was all so sad. Nothing this couple could have done, other than gambling their money away at a casino, could have given them as disappointing a result as what they were getting from their GICs. The worst mutual fund in the world could not have treated them more horribly, and Mr. and Mrs. Johnson were in dire straits. They had played into their own fears, which told them that "to buy shares in a bank might be dangerous, but to buy GICs or Canada Savings Bonds, and live on the interest, we'll be safe."

What could I do for a couple in the twilight of their years on this earth? I explained to them that there was always a possibility that we could have a stock market correction, and that they should not panic if there was one. I told them that I could not practise any kind of "market timing," because I didn't believe in that and had no idea if or when it would go down. And then I suggested that they invest in a quality mutual fund which handled a portfolio of superior businesses, such as bank stocks, Bombardier, Canwest Global, Trimark, Coca-Cola, Amex, Berkshire Hathaway, and others of that quality.

I have been thinking of that couple as I work on this chapter, because they fit so perfectly — and so pathetically — into a theory I have long held about investing. It goes like this: Every reader of this book must imagine that you, today, are confronting your own self, when you will be in your late middle age (65, 70, etc.). So there you are — 25, 35, 50, or whatever your age is, at the moment you are reading this — meeting your own self, when you will be 45, 35, or 20 years older.

I don't know how to make this any less painful, so I'll scream it out again: *You are the custodian of the older man or woman.* So you'd better have some pretty good answers to his or her awkward, and possibly mortifying, questions.

Here are some possibilities of what might transpire, for many of us:

Your older self: It's good to meet you.

You, today: Uh, well, it's good to meet you, too.

Your older self: Thanks for giving up smoking.

You, today: It was easy, really. I'm just sorry I didn't do it a lot earlier.

Your older self: Okay, let's get down to business. So, how much money have you put away for me?

You, today: Geez. Look, I . . .

Your older self: I mean, what's my net worth now? You've

had several decades to invest, you know. Did you prepare for my — hell, for *our* — future? Where's the nest egg? Will I be able to live in the way to which I was accustomed, as the divorce lawyers like to insist on behalf of their clients? Where are the investments?

You, today: Listen, please! Do you know the cost of a house in a Canadian city nowadays? What it cost to feed and clothe those kids? And now that they are heading off to university . . .

Your older self: I'm devastated. I'm sick at heart. Did you *never* think of me when you were starting out? Didn't you know that I was inside you? What could you have been thinking? Or were you even thinking at all?

The point of my playlet is abundantly clear: The vast majority of everything you earn does, of course, belong to you, but you are the custodian of the 65- or 70-year-old person within you, and if you do not put aside at least 10% of your income for this individual you have robbed him or her. You have spent that older person's money — and no excuses will be sufficient.

There's a witty bumper sticker that I've seen on dozens of cars over the past decade, which reads, "We Are Busy Spending Our Children's Inheritance." Well, it may be witty, when it comes to your children (although I personally doubt that, if you think deeply about it; don't we all wish to leave our children something, to make their lives easier than we had it?). But when the bumper sticker is applied to your older self, it becomes bitter, ugly, even heartbreaking.

Since this can get pretty depressing, I'd better turn to some advice, and quickly. There will be tons of advice in this book, but here is the perfect place to give you several real winners — five Laws of Wealth Creation that, if followed thoughtfully, will inevitably make you a winner.

Speaking of winners, I am suddenly reminded of a brilliant comment by Warren Buffett: "People would rather be offered a winning lottery ticket than a chance to get rich slowly." And I join Mr. Buffett in his belief that this truism is a very sad comment about human nature. A pretty self-destructive one, too. Okay, here goes with the Five Laws.

5

First Law of Wealth:
Pay Yourself First

THIS first law might seem a bit obvious, but like most deep thoughts, there is a lot going on here. Recall what I've been saying about how every one of us is the custodian of an older gentleman or gentlewoman of the same name who is in his or her later years of life. You haven't met that person yet, but I can assure you that the vast majority of us will feel pretty terrible when we are told that we've not done a good job with that person's net worth. If we lived beyond our means, or spent more than we earned, or did not set aside at least a portion of our income, then we have been robbing that older person who dwells in every one of us.

This is what I mean by pay yourself first. This means nothing more or less than setting aside (and investing wisely; more on that later) one-tenth to one-fifth of everything you earn, for your retirement — and from your earliest years possible.

Many years ago, I came across a story called "The Richest

Man in Babylon," and although I haven't seen it for ages it made a real impact on me and my thinking. Just the other day, I was told that a portion of this story has been reprinted in textbooks that every financial planner has to study in order to earn a licence. See if it helps you, in my retelling.

Babylon was, of course, an advanced, ancient society that existed on this earth nearly two thousand years before Christ. It had magnificent buildings, grand monuments, complex institutions. It was, inarguably, one of the most sophisticated civilizations that ever existed.

Not unlike us today, the Babylonians stored their information on hard disks — in their case, words recorded on baked clay tablets. Fortunately, several of these have been discovered in the sand, the perfect preserver of these documents.

Several hunks of clay told the story about the richest man in the great city of Babylon, whose name was Arkad, who, apparently, was the first financial planner in history. The conversation he had with a young man, if my memory serves me correctly, went something like this:

Young man: How did you come to be the richest man in all of Babylon?

Richest man: Before I answer your question, I have a few questions for you.

Young man: Very well, sir.

Richest man: Do you earn a living?

Young man: I have a job and a salary, yes.

Richest man: What do you do with that money?

Young man: Like everyone else, I suppose. I pay the rent on my home, I buy bread, shoes, clothes. . . .

Richest man: It seems to me that you are doing an

excellent job of spending your income on the goods
and services that are provided by all of those people in
our community. Indeed, you are helping to make them
all wealthy, since they are all in business to make money,
right?

Young man: I suppose so. . . .

Richest man: But what are you doing for yourself?

Young man: What on earth do you mean, sir?

Richest man: Quite simple, really: What are you
paying yourself?

Young man: Why, nothing, of course. I'm busy
paying everyone else!

I don't recall if there was anything else on that tablet, but
there is really nothing more needed to make the point. That
man did not become the richest man in Babylon by accident,
I can assure you. Here is probably the earliest document in
history of prudent, thoughtful financial planning. And this
"law," if you wish, remains fundamental to all investing to
this very day, several thousand years after they were (quite
literally) set in stone: Pay Yourself First. Otherwise, you will
pay everyone else first — whether it be for light bills, heat-
ing, car payments, gas, whatever — and end up making
everyone else in the world wealthy, and never doing the
same thing for yourself.

This leads me to two of those questions we often ask ourselves when we are very young: Why am I here on this earth?
Why do I exist? But then we get so caught up in pubescence,
school, university, love, marriage, having children, working,
and a thousand other things that we rarely confront these
questions again.

The Big Questions we must ask here are, Why do we work? — and, not unrelated, Why do businesses exist?

Think about the latter for a moment. Why is your (friendly neighbourhood) bank — whether the Royal, the Bank of Montreal, Chase Manhattan, or something else — in business? Why are Esso and Petrocan in business? Why are General Motors, Ford, Chrysler, and Honda in business?

The answer is incredibly simple, since it's for one reason only: To create wealth for their shareholders, and to maximize that wealth.

The next Big Question soon follows: How do they create that wealth for their shareholders? The answer to this query is a bit more complicated and depends on the kind of business. In the case of the banks, by taking your savings and lending it to other people who will pay good interest for it, which in turn creates wealth for their shareholders. As for the oil companies and the auto makers, it is by buying petroleum at one price and selling it at a higher price, and by convincing you that your miserable car is outdated and you really need a new one.

In life, these questions demand far more complex answers: We exist to love, to create families, to help our communities, to spiritually connect with others and with our Creator, to try to have an effect on our loved ones, and sometimes even on our society and world. But in the world of business, it's far more clear-cut: Businesses are in business to make money for the people who own them (whether their president, their employees, their shareholders — anyone with a stake in their success and survival).

There is something sad in the lives of the billions of people who do not have a financial interest in one or more businesses, and it can be described in a rather pathetic,

Sisyphean manner. (You must remember the tragic Greek character Sisyphus. He was condemned by the gods to roll a giant rock up the side of a tall mountain for Eternity. When the rock reached the top, it would always roll back down — forcing poor Sisyphus to start all over again.)

If you'd like to see a modern example of Mr. Sisyphus, simply look around you. The vast majority of people are very much like the young questioner of "The Richest Man in Babylon," are they not? They work out of the need to purchase bread so they can sustain themselves, to go to work, to buy bread to sustain themselves, to go to work, to buy bread to sustain themselves, to go to work . . . You get the idea.

This was an awful experience for the ancient Greek Sisyphus, and it is, alas, a similarly awful experience for the vast majority of humanity. The great French existentialist philosopher Albert Camus once wrote an essay about that tragic hero, concluding that he must "make believe he is happy." But I believe that most of us would prefer a more attractive kind of existence during our brief stay on this earth.

This is where the First Law of Wealth — that you must pay yourself first — comes in. Because only by paying ourselves first — and through wise financial planning that flows directly from this single fact — can we avoid a Sisyphean existence.

Yes, only through paying ourselves first, and setting aside a regular chunk of money — no matter how small that chunk is — will that magical component of Compound Interest Over Time take care of the size of that investment. Only in this way can one break the deadly cycle of work-bread-work-bread, etc. And when this cycle of working-just-to-sustain-ourselves is shattered, one may replace it with one, legitimate, crucial goal that we all have, but too rarely achieve: financial freedom. That is what paying yourself first is really all about.

Okay, now. Another quick quiz. What are the three things that any person can do with his or her money?

I'm being rhetorical here; here's the easy answer: The only three things that one can do with money are these:

- lend it,
- spend it, or
- invest it.

You have probably guessed by now which one I propose for all readers of this book, if you wish to avoid pushing giant financial boulders up giant mountains for the rest of your lives. (And you already know what happens when the rock reaches the top. It's a tough world out there.)

To be blunt, the choice is yours, no matter how strapped you find yourself at this moment, what with rent or mortgage, kids' clothes or schoolbooks, job security or even job searches. Let's look at each possibility for a moment.

Lending

If you lend it, you do not get invited to any "bondholders' meetings." No, there is simply no such thing. Only shareholders get those fancy meetings, where they get to eat caviar and enjoy the benefits of being a stakeholder among other shareholders in this or that business.

Bondholders — who have (foolishly) chosen to lend their money to a bank or a government — are paid only a medium rate of interest. (As the great American TV comic Ernie

Kovacs once noted, "They call television a 'medium' because it's not rare, and it's not well done." The same can be said about the rate of interest of bonds.)

Let's be honest here. The day that you can lend your money to a government or an institution and make a better return than you could by investing that same money in the stock of that institution is the day that business would stop being in business. To put this another way, if you choose to lend your money to, say, the Royal Bank, and you actually earn more money than you did from investing in the Royal's stock, the bank would have no reason to exist. Please remember my thought, stated above, about why any business is in business: to generate profits and to create wealth for its shareholders. And the way banks accomplish this is, of course, by taking someone's savings (or lending of money, if you wish) and lending it to others at a profit.

When the Shakespearean character Polonius lectures his son Laertes in the play *Hamlet* and pompously declares, "Neither a borrower nor a lender be," he knows what he is talking about, even if much of his other advice is pretty stupid. Lending is a fool's game — even if every bank, trust company, and insurance agency spends millions on advertising to try to talk you into doing it. Ignore all their pleas; they are only doing what businesses have to do to stay in business — make money.

Please. Let them make their money from someone else — if you don't wish to betray the 65- or 70-year-old person you will become.

So much for the first thing a person can do with money — lend it. I say, don't do it. The banks can manage just fine without you, I promise.

Spending

The second thing one can do with one's money, spend it, is self-evident. We all must spend, and living in a consumer-driven society we are all constantly reminded — by tens of thousands of commercials every single day, from TV to radio to giant billboards to the ubiquitous sides of buses and subways — of our moral obligation to spend. (As the old joke goes, "Money can't buy you happiness; it can only buy you the things that can make you happy.") We are forced to spend on goods and services from companies in the business of making money for their shareholders.

I am not about to tell people not to spend their money, especially after they've shelled out a sizeable sum to buy this book. And I suspect that most readers would agree that it's a lot more fun to live in a nice apartment or house than it is to survive inside an old refrigerator carton on a cold city street. So go and spend. But don't spend everything — which leads me to the third thing we can do with money: Invest it.

Investing

When one invests, especially in quality businesses, whether through common stocks or trustworthy mutual funds, one is actually purchasing a chunk — no matter how tiny — in those businesses, which is precisely how businesses grow, and how we all grow wealthier and better able to care for that older man or woman whom we will inevitably become.

And the best single way to invest is — you guessed it — to pay yourself first. Which leads us to our Second Law of Wealth Creation.

6

Second Law of Wealth:
Set Goals

G OALS are nice things to have, as Wayne Gretzky will be happy to tell you; he was making over $5 million U.S. a year (and far more than that, when you include his many endorsements) scoring them, until he retired in 1999. And the endorsements continue, of course. But most of you are aware that the famous hockey player had a father who would sprinkle water on his backyard every winter, put his then-toddler-aged son into tiny skates, making him go through hours of practice to teach him how to reach (well, to score) those profitable goals.

The same goes for financial goals, of course. Nebulous goals such as "I wanna be rich" are not what I'm talking about here. I'm suggesting that everyone should set goals that will define what our wealth is, and will be in the future.

Assuming that you are presently reading this book in the comfort of your home in the evening — and there is nothing good on TV anyway — let me talk about how you got to work this morning. You may think of it as a simple goal, but you still had to go through quite a bit of planning in order to achieve it.

- You knew that you had to be at the office by, say, 8:45 a.m.
- You decided how you would get there: car, train, bus, bicycle, rollerblading, jogging, whatever.
- You decided on the time you had to leave your home in order to get to work.
- You chose what route you would take.
- You had already figured out the amount of time you needed to brush your teeth, shower, shave, get dressed, and grab some kind of breakfast, and possibly even put together a lunch as well.

Not bad! You really *do* know how to set goals, don't you?

You can already see what I'm getting at here, and the examples I have used are clearly related to the Second Law of Wealth. In thoughtful financial planning, it is essential, when you set your goals about your present and future money needs, to know which route to take, and what vehicle you should use, to help you arrive at your proper financial destination. (And *when* — having to be at work by 8:45 a.m. is a lot less complex than your ultimate goal of achieving financial stability at 60, 65, 70, or whenever.)

Instead of "car" or "subway," I'm referring to such "financial vehicles" as mutual funds, publicly traded securities, limited partnerships, and so on; any or all could play a role in "getting you to your final financial destination at the proper time."

Please bear with me as I get a bit dramatic here. I would rather stick needles in my eyes than lend any of my money to a government (read "Canada or U.S. Savings Bonds") or an institution (read "bank" or "trust company"), through buying a bond or a term deposit. (At least when you stuff money into your mattress, you may be able to get a good night's sleep from the additional softness.) And, as you may have suspected, I am against anyone, especially myself, sticking needles into their eyes. Almost as heartily as I frown upon foolish, money-wasting "loans" of any kind.

You already know what I do favour and what I urge — no, beg — all readers to move towards in their lives: achieving business ownership through purchase of quality equities (i.e., stocks).

Let's play with this goal-setting concept for a while.

I could give hundreds of pages of examples, but let's try just one or two. There is a gentleman who is 50 years old this year, and he hopes to retire in 15 years, with an annual income of $50,000 a year. Problem: If there is inflation of 5% a year — please recall when it hit over 12% annually back in the late 1970s, so that's not an outrageous assumption, in spite of the low inflation rate in the late 1990s — this individual will actually need $104,000 a year in 15 years in order to purchase the same goods and services that his dreamed-of $50,000 a year was buying him a decade and a half earlier.

This means that the gentleman must have a nest egg of over $1,000,000 in order to take out that $104,000.

But which of us knows what we have to accomplish in order to achieve the financial goal of having one million dollars stashed away 15 years from today?

Very, very few of us. Using traditional vehicles, one would have to set aside in excess of $42,000 after tax at 7% after tax, and you've got your million bucks. The problem is that most people simply cannot afford to save $3000 to $4000 each year after tax, let alone $42,000.

I could give countless other examples, but I'm sure this one is sufficient.

There is a good expression that captures the Second Law of Wealth extremely well: "If you fail to plan, you plan to fail."

How true.

7

Third Law of Wealth:
Be a Contrarian

WE always complain when our children are "contrary," but I urge everyone to go the "contrarian" route when it comes to investing and amassing wealth.

Remember poet Robert Frost's famous line about "taking the road less traveled"? (It "made all the difference," he notes at the end of that poem.) Think about driving along a congested highway. You listen to the traffic reports over the radio, which warn you of overturned tractor-trailers, crowded roads, and endless traffic jams. So you (finally) decide to beat the traffic by pulling off the highway and quite literally — if not literarily — take the road less travelled. You now drive along side roads or streets that are not clogged with other people's cars. And you realize at once that you are moving faster than ever (even if the speed limit is a lot less than that on that misnamed super-highway you had been stuck on), because there's hardly anyone else on that road. Pretty smart, eh?

The above is, I feel, an excellent metaphor for the contrarian way of investing. If you take that less-travelled road in investing, you'll be a lot better off — and you'll reach your ultimate destination (in the financial case, money-freedom, or a more lucrative retirement) much, much faster.

If you do what everybody else does — whether driving on a major thoroughfare or investing in the same manner as most others — you will end up like everybody else. And that just isn't good enough.

Think of the major societies of the world over the past several thousand years. (We've already covered Babylon, if only briefly.) There is no question that the Chinese — inventors of fireworks, al dente vegetables, MSG, and countless other major creations (as well as being the most capitalistic people in the world at this moment in history) — are people of a remarkable, admirable civilization. How interesting it is, then, that they have known for millennia that the contrarian approach is the wisest way to go.

The Real Nature of Crisis

I take, as Exhibit A, the Chinese written symbol for "crisis," which is pronounced "un-geh." There are two hieroglyphs, or characters, that make up that often-frightening word, each different. One says "Danger!" and the other says "Opportunity!"

Now, isn't that a most fascinating linkage of words? The Chinese equation is, to put it in mathematical form, extremely informative: Crisis = Danger + Opportunity. Who could argue with that? I, being non-Chinese, have my own, not-unrelated expression, that your attitude determines your altitude. Let me put this another way. While most people — investors, especially — tend to focus on danger when they encounter a crisis, the true investor — the wise, thoughtful, and ultimately successful investor — focuses on opportunity.

What do I mean by this? That the successful investor actually welcomes volatility in the stock market, in the real estate market, and in every other situation, whereas that very up-and-down, uncertain situation is usually what sends the vast majority of investors focusing only on the danger aspect and heading for the hills (after stupidly dumping their stocks and mutuals just as they were leaving town).

But not you, Dear Reader. You are aware, as the great Chinese people have been aware since before the time of Christ — indeed, from even before the Babylonians — that crisis often can be dangerous, but that it, inevitably, always carries with it great opportunity. Which is why you, from the moment you read this, will stop this idiotic, self-destructive (and more to the point, financially destructive) preoccupation with the danger in every crisis (be it stock market "correction" or even stock market "crash") and focus on the opportunities those crises offer.

I talk a lot about the remarkable Berkshire Hathaway company in this book, and with good reason. During the Gulf War crisis in 1992 (yes, there's that word "crisis" again), Warren Buffett's company fell from $8900 a share to $5600. My best friend, Graham Downer, who owned two McDonald's restaurants in Cambridge, Ontario, saw "opportunity" rather than "danger" in those falling share prices, and he purchased many shares at $5600.

My friend must now feel great pleasure when he sees those same shares, just a few short years later, worth nearly

$60,000 each. But think of the anguish and even the rage of the people who panicked, and sold their Berkshire Hathaway shares at low prices, and now witness how this extraordinary company has shot back up and beyond, in spades, clubs, diamonds, and aces. Where my buddy Graham saw "opportunity" in what was obviously a crisis in the market and in that majestic stock, countless others saw only the "danger" and dumped their shares the way you would a poisoned apple.

The Report on Business of the *Globe and Mail* interviewed my friend in the fall of 1996, and the article is well worth quoting at length since his opinions capture so well what I am trying to teach in this book.

Forget Instant Gratification

Graham Downer has accumulated significant wealth by doing his bit to instantly satisfy the cravings of Canada's hungry. Now he's intent on making his portfolio grow by personally avoiding any temptation for instant financial gratification.

"The stock market is just too emotional and responds too much to things that don't have any meaning to the value of a company," says the 51-year-old owner of two McDonald's restaurants in his home town of Cambridge, Ontario.

Mr. Downer says he became a long-term, buy-and-hold investor six years ago, and it's been rewarding him with stellar gains of 20 per cent to 25 per cent a year ever since. "I became a disciple of Warren Buffett and took what he says about buying and holding good companies to heart."

One of his very first long-term bets was mutual fund

giant Trimark Financial Corp. "I bought it at around $12, and adjusted for splits it's probably around $100.". . .

Mr. Downer is also a keen buyer of mutual funds, which make up the bulk of his portfolio. He was an early investor in the AIC Advantage Fund, a Canadian equity fund that invests in shares of mutual fund managers and financial companies. He bought in at $12.42 a unit in 1991, and the units are now around $40. [In late 1999, the price was closer to $60.]

The fund has a one-year return to Aug. 31 of just over 50 per cent, and a 10-year compound annual return of 14.2 per cent. He bought into the AIC Value Fund, a U.S. equity fund, in 1990 at $7.82. The units are now around $27.75. The fund has a five-year compound return of 19.2 per cent. [In late 1999, each share of AIC Value was in the $40 range.]

His returns are amplified by the use of borrowed money. One of his trading accounts is margined up to 20 per cent. He also has a leveraged account, funded by a bank loan, with the investments in the account serving as security. "I see it as optimizing opportunities to create wealth," he says.

Before his conversion to long-term investing, Mr. Downer admits having met his share of losses trying to pick overnight successes. "I was jumping in and out of the market using my heart, not my head," he says.

His worst move in recent years — buying Republic Waste Industries Inc. (controlled at the time by former Laidlaw Inc. chief Michael Degroote) in 1991 — was when he abandoned his buy-and-hold beliefs. "I went to this big hyped-up marketing meeting, and got all caught up in the excitement," he recalls. "I put in around $40,000 and it proceeded to go to half of that, and I sold it."

Still, he says, those occasional lapses renew his faith in the buy-and-hold approach. "I get burnt, shake myself and go back to what works."

His advice to others: "Buy companies with good management and good track records, and hold them for a long period of time," he says.

"My biggest advice is patience, patience, patience."

Along with a photograph of Graham is what newspaper people call a sidebar, a piece including other quotations from the investor. Under "best advice," my friend is quoted as declaring, "You have to be patient and not get emotional. You can't look at this stuff every day — it just drives you crazy." (I agree, and will have more to say about this later.)

What makes people panic? Why do some people put on boxing gloves while others turn tail? (I believe that scientists refer to this as the "fight or flight" syndrome, and it may well be built into our nervous systems, going back millions of years.)

I certainly do not understand why so many people choose to "handle" crises or seeming disaster by selling off their best investments; that may well be for a registered psychiatrist to consider and explain. But I do know this much. When there is a crisis, it is the best time in the world to invest. One should not fear it. On the contrary, it should be welcomed.

Why? That's a perfectly understandable question. When stocks fall precipitously, is that not the time to cut bait? To "save what you can"? To "get out while the getting is good"? (It's not by chance that there are so many clichés about this action; it's a very popular — if not particularly clever — road to take.)

I'll tell you why *not*. Because when there is a crisis — be it war in the Gulf, Quebec threatening to separate from Canada, the death of a political leader, tensions in the Middle East — it is inevitably accompanied by wonderful opportunities.

What kind of wonderful opportunities? To buy up great stocks at low prices. To buy good businesses. To start your own business. To purchase real estate. To buy any assets at low, discount prices. (Or maybe you prefer always to pay full price?)

But that's not the way that the masses act, is it? No, they behave irresponsibly and irrationally — and the key word here is the latter, "irrationally" — and sell off great investments or quality businesses at absurd prices. And we really do know why, don't we? Because they see only see the Chinese character for "danger," and they ignore the same-sized word "opportunity," hidden in that same, scary word, "crisis."

As you can see, being a contrarian is crucial, because it always tells you the wisest time to invest: when others are heading for the exit doors.

You know the ones who are painting the word "exit" in larger and brighter letters every single day: the newspapers and magazines. Most people, alas, get much of their investment knowledge from the daily paper. And the majority of newspapers tell people such uninspired (and jump-on-the-bandwagon) things as how we should all "invest now" — or soon after everyone else has done so; true, the price of those shares is high, but then that's because they are so hot. (And to think that we humans actually feel superior to lemmings, as they follow each other off cliffs.)

It is to laugh — or to weep. While the great stock market cliché is "buy low, sell high," it seems as if the entire world conspires to urge us to "buy high" (when everyone else is buying, and pushing those shares up in price), and only then to "sell low." (As you panic and hurry to dump your shares, terrified by the inevitable newspaper headlines that scream "Market Tumbles for Second Straight Day!")

My attitude — and altitude, if I say so myself — is similar to that of Warren Buffett and Berkshire Hathaway: If you can, buy low and (much, much later) sell high. And even if you can't buy low, then at least buy excellent businesses at reasonable prices — and then hold on to them. (And don't dump them at the first sign of market hysteria, which is, alas, inevitable.)

Market Timing

This discussion of crises brings me to the topic of market timing, which is the subject of many a book. It's very informative that there are no billionaires in the Forbes 400 Richest People listings who are market timers; they are all prudent business owners. I don't really know of any individuals who have made money on market timing, because sooner or later they will make an incorrect move, and give back the money. It's all guesswork; it's all garbage.

Not so the contrarian investor. He or she knows that the best prices to be had are when markets are going through turmoil. You don't have to look back any further, at least in Canada, than the days following the failure of the ill-fated Meech Lake Accord, or the Charlottetown Accord (or was it Discord?), or the squeaky-close Quebec Referendum of

1995. In the U.S., it can be anything from political assassination to Senate scandal to race riots to international war jitters.

I'll say this several times in this book, but it bears repeating: Meech Lake may collapse, but billions of people will still reach for a Coke the following day. The Charlottetown Accord may fall apart, but billions will still have to shave the next morning with a Gillette razor, to paraphrase Warren Buffett. True, the fine Canadian firm of Bombardier is located in the province of Quebec, but you don't need to possess a doctorate in political science to know that if Quebec becomes hostile, or, sadly, even if it becomes independent, that company will simply pick up and move elsewhere, seeking out a friendlier environment. And no number of failed constitutional conferences or even independent provinces will prevent people, whether they be Canadian, American, or European, from buying their Ski-Doos, Jet Skis, corporate aircraft, and the many other superior products that Bombardier manufactures, markets, and sells so brilliantly. And the most dreadful political upheavals in the United States, the UK, or Europe will not prevent the average man or woman in each country from pulling on Levi's jeans, sliding into Nike shoes, and heading off to grab a hamburger and soft drink at the nearest McDonald's.

No, what the contrarian is concerned with are the earnings of each business, not external crises, which, more often than not, fade away as surely as the morning dew. The true contrarian is an opportunist who recognizes that every crisis produces more than danger. And rather than be negative, he or she focuses on the opportunity that invariably presents itself at the same, difficult time.

Indeed, this problem of "predicting the market" is worth a section all its own.

It's Not Timing the Market — It's Time *in* the Market

Timing can be crucial whether you are a married couple who wishes to conceive a child or a basketball team with a two-point lead (or deficit) with 10 seconds left to go in the fourth quarter of the game.

But one of the things I am forever telling my clients is this: It is impossible to predict the stock market. And even if we could, it is ultimately irrelevant. And by irrelevant, I mean precisely that. Predicting the market is totally, completely, 100% irrelevant.

I talk about Coca-Cola a lot in this book, but I don't do this because it happens to make up such a large percentage of Warren Buffett's Berkshire Hathaway portfolio. Please recall what I mentioned earlier about Coke's share-price movement over the past several years — from the year 1980, to be precise. Since that year, the common stock of Coca-Cola has grown by an average of 28% per annum. And don't forget that an investment of $100,000 in Coca-Cola shares in that year would grow to become, by late 1999, over $6.5 million dollars. (And, since you might not have had $100,000 to invest some two decades ago, then try it this way. If you had invested a mere $10,000 in shares of Coke in 1980, you'd now be in possession of well over half a million dollars. Still pretty impressive.)

But I'm not talking here about *what you should have done*; I'm talking about the absurdity of *trying to predict the market*. Since you (and I) failed to make that brilliant investment in Coca-Cola, a lot has happened in the world. The federal government of Canada has gone from Liberal to Conservative to Liberal; the presidency of the United States has see-sawed from Democratic to Republican to Democratic; the federal deficits of both countries have skyrocketed; there have been constant political crises in the former Soviet Union, the Middle East, and Africa; totalitarian governments have fallen across Eastern Europe and Russia, as did the Berlin Wall; there was a frightening — or was it? — "stock market crash" in Canada, the United States, and around the globe in the fall of 1987; and interest rates have gone from towering, even usurious heights down to the lowest numbers in half a century (at least in the fall of 1999, as I write these words).

To paraphrase a famous banking song, the times, they've been a-changin'. Yes, the world has changed quite a bit since 1980. Yet did you come across many newspaper or magazine articles that predicted any of these crises? Neither did I. All they did was report what happened in the world — after it happened.

Yet all the while that the USSR was shattering into a dozen pieces; that Romania's long-time dictator was tortured and then shot by his former subjects; that Israel invaded Lebanon, had its prime minister assassinated and several of its public buses blown up; that all of us shuddered (and probably dumped our stocks by the billions of shares) as the market fell so "precipitously" in October 1987; that O.J. Simpson did (or didn't) murder his wife and her friend — Coca-Cola shares continued to climb (with the occasional "correction," of course), by an average of over 25% every single frightening, unsure, hit-and-miss, unpredictable year.

Nostradamus did a pretty impressive job, back in the Rennaissance, of mystically and mysteriously predicting world wars, assassinations, and social upheavals that would not occur until many centuries after he died, but I wouldn't play the market by his writings, any more than by the scribblings of the most esteemed stock market timer. No individual has the ability to successfully predict the future. Therefore, we should not pay any attention to things over which we have no control.

No — I take that back: I'd like to make one fearless prediction — and I can be far more confident of the correctness of my prediction than any Nostradamus or Jeanne Dixon of the past, present, or future. I here predict that the earnings of Coca-Cola will continue to grow, and will be much greater by the year 2001 than they are in the fall of 1999.

Now, how can I possibly make such a fearless, reckless prediction? Well, because in the countries where 650 million people live, Coca-Cola sells over 150 million soft drink servings every year. Yet in the areas where another 4.5 billion people now live, Coca-Cola sells less than 10 soft drink servings each year.

And how about India, which is closing in on one billion people? In poor, overcrowded India, Coke sells less than 2. And ever-more-affluent China, with its 1.3 billion people? Also less than 2 servings each year.

My heavens! What if our Indian friends start to drink 4 or 8 servings a year? What if our Chinese neighbours start to drink 5, 10, 20, even 50 servings a year?

There are so many things that could happen over the coming decades. Hurricanes, floods, and earthquakes. Peace could break out in the Middle East. All those Serbs and

Croats and Bosnians could all reunite in a joyously resurrected Yugoslavia. Well, maybe not that.

Inarguably, anything is possible in the future.

But I can tell you what is probable. That there will be a dramatic rise in the value of Coca-Cola shares so huge that our heads will collectively spin. Of course, there will always be those — probably 90% of shareholders — who will far too eagerly sell their shares over the next few years, happily "taking their profits" but thereby giving up the potential of seeing their savings double, triple, and even more. And at an average 25% increase in Coca-Cola's share prices every year since 1980 — and without the thirst of over two billion people in China and the Indian subcontinent — it won't take very long for that doubling, tripling, and even more to occur.

No one can predict the market. No one. But with a little bit of research into quality businesses, you can do rather well — providing that you are not self-destructive with your investment decisions. (More on that below.)

Being a "contrarian" means that you must be passionately committed to three major beliefs — all of which, interestingly, radiate more common sense that 90% of the beliefs of non-contrarian investors. Here they are, one by one:

1. You must be a business owner.

And I mean be a business owner, regardless of what you actually "do" in your life and career. If you are presently running a business (whether bike repair or baking bread, that's not my concern), then you have already achieved this. It is not by chance that, in every part of the world, the richest people are those who own businesses.

But even if you do not see yourself as a "business

owner," you become one when you invest in common stocks. So, if you are a civil servant, own a business, or at least a tiny chunk of a business, through shares in a company you trust. If you are a doctor, do the same. Or a teacher. Even if you are an unemployed labourer, somehow find the money (more on that as well, below) and do it.

You must have commitment to business ownership if you wish to grow and prosper. (And buying and selling shares in countless different companies, jumping from ownership to ownership like a kangaroo on steroids, is not what I am talking about here.)

2. Make sure that you own an excellent business with wonderful, long-term economic fundamentals.
Every business, much like every person, is not necessarily decent, reliable, trustworthy, with growth potential. When you "own" (invest in) a business, you should own only those domiciled in strong, long-term growth industries, and run by honest, shareowner-oriented managements.

3. Your share-ownership in that business you "own" should be permanent.
I do not mean "permanent" in the way that your hairdresser does, since those "permanents" usually last only a few weeks or months. I mean precisely the opposite of what 95% of all "players" in the stock markets and mutual funds do. You must actually buy and hold your "ownership" of that business (or businesses), in the way that most of our grandparents married, and truly believed in the words "for better or for worse, for richer or poorer, in sickness and in health . . ." This metaphor works surprisingly well,

because which business has not had its better days and its worse days; which business has not been richer on some days and poorer on others; which business has never been sick or healthy?

The fantastic success of Warren Buffett, and other great investors to whom I refer in this book, is due not so much to what they have done as to what they have not done. They have not sold their investments. They have not taken any profits. They have not flitted from stock to stock to stock like starving bumblebees or butterflies.

These men and women never say, "Look! The market is high this week. I'd better sell my shares now, because the market will undoubtedly fall, and I can always buy back in." They have done the simplest thing possible, not unlike a business owner who nurtures his business through good times and bad, by paying careful attention to the fundamentals. They have purchased quality businesses (or shares in them) and held on for the long haul, because they had faith in the worth of those businesses — and have not gone for the immediate gratification of making "a killing on the stock market." And who of us has not heard a friend say, "Guess how well I did! I bought a thousand shares of X at $XX, just a few months ago, and I just dumped them at $XXX, for a profit of $XX,XXX. Not bad, eh?"

Actually, I think it's plenty bad, and terribly risky, and pretty stupid — and this book will show you why this is so.

The Real Action

But now it's time for one of my favourite analogies, which I heard from one of the great investors whom I respect and admire (I'm sure he'll forgive my paraphrase): "Keep your eyes focused on the playing field."

What do I mean by this?

It's simple and logical, really. Imagine that you and a friend have gone to a ball game — baseball, football, basketball, hockey, whatever. Your friend keeps his eyes firmly fastened on the scoreboard.

"Look, we're ahead," he says at one point.

"Oh, no! We've fallen behind," he says a little later.

"Look at the score now. We're never gonna catch up."

And so on, ad nauseum.

Your friend may be a very good friend and a fine husband and father, but he is an idiot, at least in this situation. You are both attending a competition, and all the important, crucial action — the stuff that counts — is right out there on the diamond, the playing field, the court, the ice. And your buddy has chosen to keep his eyes firmly fixed on that stupid scoreboard.

This analogy makes a tremendous amount of sense. When a person goes to a sports event, one does not spend all one's time focused on the scoreboard. One should — nay, must — look at the playing field — because what's happening on that playing field is what eventually puts the numbers up on the scoreboard. Of course we all like to look up at the scoreboard — occasionally — to see who's ahead, who's behind. But it is obviously the playing field where all eyes should be riveted.

If you haven't figured out the connection by now, here it is in living black and white. The stock market is the scoreboard. And the playing field is the businesses themselves.

Now, when you are investing in publicly traded securities or mutual funds, it's nice to know, occasionally, how they are doing, but you certainly want to spend very little of your time staring at the stock market pages/scoreboard. They are irrelevant.

It is what is happening to the business — its profits and losses, its sales and its breakthroughs and its setbacks and its plans for the future — that is truly important.

Naturally, the man or woman who knows the batting average of a particular baseball player against a certain pitcher, or against left-handed or right-handed pitchers, or how well he hits when there are men on base, and his strike-out percentages, has a lot more fun at the ballpark than the person (or politician) who believes that the Dodgers are still in Brooklyn.

The same with the thoughtful person who keeps his or her eyes on the business/playing field. One should do everything possible to further understand the business, through attending shareholder meetings, reading annual reports, following management machinations and plans. To ignore how a business is doing (or not to watch the players on the field) is to endanger one's investment, not to mention pleasure. A business owner (i.e., an investor in a business or businesses) must pay attention to the business fundamentals, and not focus on the often silly, usually irrational movements of the stock market. (After all, most investors are self-destructive and greedy, as we know so well, usually from personal experience.)

A brief example of the scoreboard/playing field analogy,

linked with a major Canadian business, could be helpful here. Most of you are probably familiar with Magna International, the magnificently successful auto-parts maker, co-founded and built into a billion-dollar firm by Frank Stronach. The stock price of Magna began to fall like a stone several years ago, after Mr. Stronach stepped down, even though the company continued to put several hundreds of dollars in parts into every single car built in North America. One week it sold for over $30 (on the scoreboard known as the Toronto Stock Exchange); within months it was hovering around the $2 range.

Investors dumped Magna shares by the millions — and who could blame them? They watched the scoreboard/stock market pages daily; they saw their investment crumbling like Miss Havisham's wedding cake. Yet Magna continued to manufacture auto parts by the tens of millions, and sales continued to grow around the world.

Stronach came back and took over the reins of his beloved company once again, and the stock began to shoot up in a surprisingly short period of time: $4, $8, $20, $40 — up to the $80 range in late 1999. Those who watched only the scoreboard got badly burned; those who kept their eyes on the playing field (Magna's sales, its factories, its expansion, its leader's return to the running of the company) did quite a bit better, wouldn't you agree?

This leads me to one further point about the success of the contrarian approach.

Forget Las Vegas–Style Investing

One of the worst, most treacherous clichés in the world of investing is "buy low and sell high." This is nonsense, and it never works consistently. Even worse, it leads to Las Vegas–type gambling, and not the true investing that I am urging throughout this book. The line should actually read, "buy and hold."

People forget that the only way to get stocks when they are truly low-priced is when there is a crisis (and you have not forgotten already, I trust, my Chinese equation of Crisis = Danger + Opportunity). War breaks out in an oil-producing country? Ten million oranges freeze on the trees of central Florida? Something is always happening to make investors panic (and, yes, self-destruct), which allows us brilliant contrarians to leap in and "buy low."

The key to being a contrarian is to recognize that you are only going to get a truly "good" price when other people are selling. And you already know why they are selling like mad; because of their own, irrational (read "self-destructive") behaviour. Those poor souls (and we've all been one of them, let's face it) are dumping their securities at foolishly low prices because they are terrified that their net worth will drop to zero.

But if you have been investing in an excellent, quality, top-notch, well-positioned business, you don't have to worry. Of course, stock markets and stock prices and mutual funds will fluctuate, often even hourly, but — over time — nothing on the face of the earth will ever give you what a superior, publicly traded security will give you, with the possible exception of your own, personally run business.

Ever notice what happens in the newspapers and magazines when the stock market suddenly turns bearish? The headlines never read "Now Is the Time to Invest," do they? No, they read "Banks Mired in Depression." "Trust Companies

Fear Bankruptcy." "Businesses Expect Dreadful Future in Crumbling Marketplace." "Stocks Fall Faster than Michael Jackson's Reputation."

I remember reading headlines like these during the major recession of the early 1980s and once again through late October and November 1987. And I also remember what most people have long forgotten: That even in that frightening, death-defying year of 1987, the average stock on the Standard & Poor's 500 still rose over 5% during those 12 months — and then continued to rise another 16%+ in the following 12 months. Some Crash. Some Great Depression. Sir John Templeton, the admirable founder of one of the most successful collections of mutual funds of all time, once exclaimed, "Don't ask me where the outlook is good; ask me where it's the worst." He went on to add, "You see, it's where the outlook is worst, and when blood is in the streets, that one is going to get the very best prices. Because when you are dealing with publicly traded securities, you're trying to buy at the very best price. And that will come only when there are bad times."

Let me now call upon my wonderful Jamaican heritage for a classic aphorism: "Chicken merry, hawk near." You get the picture: A chicken runs out into the farmyard, sunning her feathers, feeling euphoric and enjoying the great weather, and, inevitably, the hawk is nearby, ready to pounce.

And that's precisely what we heard throughout the fall and winter of 1996-97, as people grew euphoric about the returns they saw on their mutual funds and stocks, and how the stock market has been on a tear since 1992, and the Dow Jones soared past 6000 for the first time in history. Chicken merry, hawk near, you hear from everyone. When will it all come crashing down? When should we "get out" of this dangerously over-heated market? When will the hawk come swooping?

When, indeed.

Self-Destruction

I'm talking about self-destructive attitudes here. As I've noted, attitude determines one's altitude, and fear of poverty too often makes that poverty a reality. It is rotten attitudes (uh-oh — hawk near!) that keep so many of us from seeing the opportunity, whether in the crisis or even in the chicken-merry times.

Was it Mark Twain or Stephen Leacock who wrote that "when opportunity knocks, most people are off in a bar, drinking beer"? But even if they do hear that knocking when they are home, intensely perusing the stock market page, and ignoring the playing field, they often think, "It's too good to be true; it can't be happening to me. Can it really be Ed McMahon from the Publishers Clearing House at the door, clutching a $10 million cheque with my name on it?" (Well, probably not.)

People are simply self-destructive with their investment decisions. They don't like paying reasonable prices; they actually feel better and more clever when they are paying higher prices! I often ask my clients to view their investments in the same way that they view their supermarket shopping. In other words, when you look at the stock market, think supermarket.

When there is a great sale on toilet paper — eight rolls for the price of six — do we not tend to stock up? You know we do. When there is an exciting deal on your favourite canned soup, or canned beans, or potato chips, don't you buy as many as they will let you buy? You bet. (Sales on milk or yogurt or something perishable are different, of course; but I still see many people stocking up on ice cream if there's a great deal being offered.)

And why do nearly all of us stock up on toilet paper and canned goods at our friendly neighbourhood supermarket when there is a sale on, or a 40%-off coupon available through the mail or in the daily newspaper? We all know why: There is great pleasure that comes from looking into our pantry and declaring, if only to ourselves, "I paid $1.29 a box for that facial tissue, only last month. And here I just managed to buy a dozen boxes for only 79 cents each. How proud Mother would be if she could see me saving money like this!" It's almost visceral, this feeling of "I got a real bargain," and it's perfectly logical. After all, who likes to waste money?

The latter is not a rhetorical question, since it has a very troubling answer. Tens of millions of men and women must love to waste money, because they display this habit every single day on the stock markets of the world.

You want further examples of absurd, self-destructive behaviour? Of manic behaviour that quickly leads to depressive feelings of near despair?

Look no further than the price of gold. Remember how gold was artificially "fixed" at $35 an ounce for many decades, until it was finally freed from those constraints? It shot up — literally overnight — to $100 an ounce, $300, $500, even $800 an ounce. And when did the largest number of people leap into this doomed-to-crash hysteria? When gold hit a grotesque $900 an ounce, at which point men and women were lined up by the thousands along Bay Street in Toronto and Wall Street in New York, taking out mortgages on their houses, eager to leap on the boat when it was actually leaving the harbour.

We all know what happened: The price of gold collapsed like a cheap suitcase, and millions were wiped out. And it has rarely (if ever) broken $400 an ounce over the two decades since — during which time countless stocks of great, trustworthy companies have skyrocketed in value and price.

Here's another self-destructive tale, and one that is a lot closer to home for Canadian readers. People lined up by the thousands to buy condominiums from various builders across Canada, right through the late 1980s, especially in Toronto, when some real estate was reaching $400 a square foot. They sure aren't lining up now, are they? You can pick one up, like an overripe apple from a tree, for 50% less than those peak prices today, at the turn of the century. Just don't mention what you paid for it to your still-suffering next-door neighbour, who purchased his condo at the peak of the market, just before the whole thing crashed. Imagine how his broken heart will shatter further when he realizes that he's still got a $250,000 mortgage on that gorgeous condo, after putting up an equal amount in cash, when the market was so hot (and would clearly keep on going up forever), while you didn't put a penny down, and have a mortgage of only $200,000. But then, who ever said that life was fair? (As a witty caption reads under an advertisement of a beautiful Mercedes 500SL, "If life was fair, we'd all have one of these.")

The answer, of course, is to never jump on the bandwagon, whether that bandwagon is plugging gold, condos, or "hot" stocks. The true contrarian must view publicly traded securities as investments, not as paper to be shuffled and quickly traded or dumped. One must avoid getting involved with manias, which are the ultimate in self-destructiveness.

But what do I mean when I write "manias"? After all, many thoughtful people have claimed that the entire mutual fund "boom" is a mania.

I beg to differ. Because unlike gold, condos, or tulip bulbs in Holland several centuries ago, mutual funds are *not* a "thing"; they are a system of investing. And this system of investing has grown along with a powerful demographic shift from consumption to saving in North America, as the aging baby boomer population has become convinced that governments will probably never be able to provide them with an adequate pension.

Remember that best-selling book earlier this decade? It was called *Rotten Men and the Women Who Tolerate Them*, or something like that. I could well call this book *Self-Destructive People and the Lousy Investment Decisions They Make*. But that would be too negative, and I'm always plugging how very important it is to be positive in one's life and one's attitudes.

So let's just summarize my Third Law of Wealth by saying that if one follows the contrarian approach in purchasing shares of businesses on the stock market (as we do every week almost unconsciously at the supermarket), we will do best if we keep our eye on the playing field (and not on the scoreboard/stock market pages), purchase only quality businesses (or portions thereof), avoid manias, and stop being so dreadfully self-destructive.

And now, on to the Fourth Law.

8

Fourth Law of Wealth:
Leverage Human Resources

INTERESTINGLY, just as most people are contrarian at the supermarket (always eager to purchase consumer products at low prices), if not in the stock market, the majority of humanity is already steeped in this philosophy of leveraging human resources, if only unconsciously.

The examples come easily. You have a mechanical problem with your automobile. It keeps stalling; it's making strange and unwelcome noises; it consumes far too much gas. Do you fix it yourself? (Some do, but few of us have the ability, what with today's increasingly complex, computerized cars.) No, you hire a competent mechanic, whose job it is to know what's wrong, to find it quickly, and repair it.

Legal problem? It may drive you crazy, but you sense that it'll drive you even crazier unless you turn to a lawyer.

Let's talk actual life and death for a moment. You suddenly have chest pains (heaven forbid). Do you take a course on "open-heart surgery" at your nearby community college or Learning Annex?

I sense not. Indeed, this same ready acceptance of the wisdom of going to the experts is why we tend to turn to social workers, psychologists, and psychiatrists when we encounter family or emotional difficulties. We know, almost instinctively, that we want experts to fix our car, our legal problems, and our health, whether physical or mental. All of us have watched our own parents call a plumber or electrician when they felt they could not deal with the dilemma themselves, and we respected them for it; after all, what are professionals (and craftspeople) for, if not to fix or improve or heal what we ourselves cannot accomplish with as much skill, speed, or simple ability?

As I said, my Fourth Law of Wealth is actually part of the unconscious way that we tend to do things in our lives. Yet when it comes to personal investment, financial planning, and wealth creation — so that we do not leave that 65- or 70-year-old who lives in us all up the financial creek when he or she appears before us — how many of us "leverage" this human resource? Sadly, far too few, and the results are often tragic.

Who Is on Your Board of Directors?

Just as we turn to a medical doctor for our ills, it is essential that we turn to experts in financial dealings for our monetary present and future. I like to put it this way, to my clients: "Take a business-like approach to your personal affairs, and actually establish a board of directors." (In other words, leverage those human resources.)

Every major company has a board of directors, and the purpose of that board is singular and essential, to answer the question, How can we best bring independent thinking to management meetings, to explore ways to maximize shareholders' wealth? Down at the board meetings in Atlanta, Georgia, the board of directors of Coca-Cola has Warren Buffett sitting there, along with Peter V. Ueberroth, the president of the Sun Trust Bank of Atlanta, and many others — all of them bringing their insights into how that company can continue to thrive. I can assure you, their president, Douglas Ivester, listens open-mindedly and eagerly to his board of directors, and it's not only because the directors each happen to be wealthy enough or lucky enough to own a large number of Coca-Cola shares.

In the world of personal finance, you will want to establish your own board of directors. And to take a business-like approach, you need to surround yourself with the best thinkers and the finest financial advice available. You will therefore wish to align yourself only with those who have proven investment strategies. By electing a personal investment advisor to become your own chairman of the board, he or she will bring to you other areas of expertise and professionals in the field, along with money managers, and so on. Your automobile deserves the finest mechanic, your health the finest doctor, and your financial portfolio the finest experts and investment advisors.

Just as one would be wise to refrain from performing one's own open-heart surgery, similarly one should never take a two-week course on investment strategies and then go and run your own investments yourself. Or go to a no-load discount broker. No, you should demand a powerful investment advisor as chairman of your board of directors, who will direct you wisely and thoughtfully and keep you invested in a portfolio of superb, successful businesses for the rest of your life. I believe it is improbable that one can put into place, and keep together, a quality investment program over a lifetime without some help from a professional investment advisor.

Not unrelated to the above, read on for my Fifth Law of Wealth Creation.

9

Fifth Law of Wealth: Leverage Capital

THIS law is the one that frightens people the most, so let me attempt to allay your fears with a far more frightening declaration: It is impossible to work, pay taxes, save your after-tax income, and still manage to build up a meaningful net worth. What you're working with is simply too small an amount to begin accumulating serious money. Even when you use your RRSP to its fullest degree — and remember, it is tax-deferred, of course — your nest egg is going to be insufficient.

I cannot deny that this last law of mine is quite controversial, but being controversial does not mean that it has to be risky. One must borrow money in order to invest and build a suitable nest egg that will serve for retirement if you have needs greater than a bird's.

Before you begin to panic and close the covers of this book, think about the house in which you probably dwell.

How did you purchase that home? If you are like the vast majority of citizens of this country, indeed, of this world, you took out a mortgage to be able to afford it.

Now, most people tend to view home ownership as an investment, but this is simply not so. It is a lifestyle choice. And you would never be living in your present house had you not borrowed the money to buy it. In much the same way, unless you borrow money to invest, you will probably not have an adequate net worth.

What's almost funny about this law is that the vast majority of Canadians is incredibly eager to borrow billions of dollars to purchase consumer durables. Indeed, as I write these words at the turn of the century, there is over $500 billion in consumer debt in this country. Debt on credit cards. On car loans. On still unpaid-for fridges and stoves. On houses.

On Owning a House, or Reaching for a Coke

Many of you will not like when I say this, but it's true: Home ownership is inarguably the single greatest detriment to wealth creation in North America. The average homeowner, in slowly paying off a mortgage of several hundred thousand dollars on his or her house, ends up spending close to a million dollars in payments over several decades. Once again, home ownership is not an investment; it's simply where (and how) you choose to live. It is a utility, not wealth creation.

This will be a painful example, but I must give it. Think of the person who borrowed $100,000 as a down payment on a house in 1980, and his friend, who borrowed the same sum to purchase shares in Coca-Cola. You already know about what happened to the latter; it's worth several million dollars today, which could buy a half-dozen houses in several locations around the world, most of them a lot warmer than Canada. And the house "owner"? His house probably has gone up in value — maybe even two or three times. Let's say five times, just to be generous to the poor guy. So he now owns a house (well, he undoubtedly still has a way to go on the mortgage) that's worth half a million dollars. Big, bloody deal.

Which situation would you rather be in today? Which person did better?

My point was illustrated quite brilliantly by a journalist named Josh McHugh in the June 19, 1995, issue of *Forbes* magazine. The one-page article was wittily entitled "Why the Kennedys Aren't the Rockefellers." Essentially, the article reminded us how most of us were pretty impressed when the Kennedys sold their famous beachfront home in Palm Beach, Florida, for $4.9 million that year; after all, the family patriarch Joe Kennedy paid only $100,000 for it six decades earlier.

A fifty-fold increase in the value of the house, most of us thought to ourselves. What a great deal.

But when you reach for a calculator, you quickly realize that Joe Kennedy's $100,000, sunk into that lovely house and property in 1933, actually grew at a compound annual rate of only 6.5% over those 62 years, in order to reach the $4.9 million sale price.

To quote from the *Forbes* article: "That's about two percentage points ahead of inflation over the six decades, but it lags behind even the price appreciation of the S&P 500. We exclude here dividends on the S&P 500 (as well as taxes and upkeep on the house)."

Ah, but what if Joe Kennedy had put the same $100,000 into Standard Oil of New Jersey stock in the same year? It "would have compounded at more than 13% annually — and now be worth about $250 million in Exxon stock. Today the Rockefellers are billionaires on the Forbes Four Hundred. The centimillionaire Kennedys barely made the list last year [1994] and may not make it this year."

The journalist's conclusion? "Houses are nice to live in, but if you want to leave your heirs serious money, buy common stocks, and . . . reinvest those dividends."

Borrowing need not be scary; many individuals have borrowed money to be able to start a business. Most of us borrow to purchase houses and cars. So why not borrow money to invest thoughtfully, carefully, and creatively? Especially when one follows the first four of my Laws of Wealth: Pay yourself first. Set articulated financial goals. Be a contrarian, by ignoring the stock market and taking the road less travelled. Leverage human resources. And, of course, this last, fifth, one: Use other people's money to make more money for yourself, your retirement, your children, your future.

I was interviewed at length in the fall of 1996 by a fine journalist from Canada's largest newspaper, the *Toronto Star*. Jade Hemeon, whose column on mutual funds ran regularly in the mid-1990s, articulated my feelings about this fifth and crucial law so well that I asked her permission to quote that article, which ran in that paper on October 27 of that year, in full:

When Borrowing to Invest Makes Some Sense

With interest rates lower than they've been since the 1950s, the idea of borrowing to invest is worth considering.

Many people steer away from taking out a loan to buy mutual funds or shares for fear of risk. But the strategy should be weighed in a dispassionate manner.

After all, home buyers take on big mortgages to purchase an asset that produces no income and is often a money pit.

Others will borrow to invest in their own businesses — often a risky start-up venture. [Note from Richard Charlton: Indeed, four out of five new business fail within their first five years of existence, which are pretty frightening odds, wouldn't you say?]

Why, then, doesn't it make sense to borrow to invest in carefully selected, diversified mutual funds or companies with conservative management and superior track records?

The key is to take a long-term perspective and borrow a manageable amount, with interest payments you can easily handle. Plunging into debt up to your neck to invest in speculative securities is financial suicide, but borrowing to invest in companies with proven success is a completely different strategy.

"One of the most important laws of wealth creation is that you must use other people's money to create a nest egg of any size," says Richard Charlton . . . "With interest rates so low, borrowing makes more sense than ever."

The key, says Charlton, is to invest in the right public companies and the right mutual funds. He points to the long-term track records of consistent top performers such as Templeton Growth Fund, with a 10-year average annual return of 12 per cent, AIC Advantage Fund, with an average of 15.5 per cent over 10 years, and Trimark Fund, with 15.0 per cent.

While there are no ironclad guarantees that past returns will be repeated, a long track record is an indication that a fund manager can perform well through various types of market conditions.

With the prime rate at 5.25 per cent [as of the fall of 1996], floating-rate investment loans are available from such institutions as Canada Trust and the Bank of Montreal for as low as prime plus one-half a percentage point. The terms of loans depend on an individual's net worth, collateral and duration of the loan.

Unlike the interest on mortgages used to buy a home, the interest on an investment loan is tax deductible against income from investments. If investments don't pay enough in the form of interest or dividends to cover the loan cost, it is deductible against other income.

Stock mutual funds typically don't pay out a lot of interest and dividends, but provide the opportunity for capital gain. Capital gains are taxable in the year in which they are realized, but at a lower rate than interest and income. Capital gains taxes can be deferred by holding on to stocks for the long term, or selecting mutual funds with low portfolio turnover.

If you are in the top tax bracket, you can cut your actual after-tax interest costs by as much as half, because of the tax deductibility of interest. That could bring the after-tax cost of a 6 per cent loan as low as 3 per cent. For this strategy to succeed, your mutual funds returns need only be higher than your after-tax interest costs.

Investors must keep in mind that stocks and stock funds are volatile, and will have good years and bad. There could be some years when interest costs could exceed your investment returns. If you borrow to invest you must have the intestinal fortitude to withstand stock market corrections.

Charlton says investors must learn to view their stock investments or mutual funds in the same way as they would the purchase of a business. The idea is to buy securities for the long term, not for short-term trading profits.

Over the years, he has recommended such stocks as Gillette Co., Coca-Cola Co., Berkshire Hathaway, Trimark Investment Management, and the Canadian banks to his clients, as well as mutual funds where the managers practice a similar philosophy of buying superior businesses for the long term.

When you hold a good business, or a fund portfolio of good businesses, you are better able to resist the urge to panic and dump your holdings when the market corrects, Charlton says.

Borrowing to invest — known as leveraging — has its detractors. Among them is mutual fund guru John Templeton, who is concerned about what's known as the margin call. A margin call occurs when you have pledged your stocks and mutual funds as collateral against a loan, and the terms of that loan require a minimum percentage of equity against debt. If your investments fall drastically in value — reducing the value of your equity — you could be on the hook for more collateral to satisfy your lender. If you can't supply it, you could be forced to sell your investments in a down market.

Charlton advises his clients to minimize the risk by arranging a long-term investment loan with a lender, not short-term margin financing.

Some lenders are willing to provide long-term investment loans up to 20 years in maturity. Your mutual funds are used as collateral, but without the margin requirements — providing you have the ability to make payments and are a good credit risk. You can also borrow against a stable asset such as a fully-paid-for home. If you're borrowing to invest in stocks or funds, your interest costs are tax deductible.

A 20-year investment loan of $50,000 could be arranged at today's interest rates to provide you with payments of $240 or so a month.

Tax deductibility would reduce these interest costs significantly. But only the interest portion of a loan payment is tax deductible, and the amount of principal in the payment rises as the loan ages.

If interest rates go up, a floating rate loan could become more expensive and you might find yourself facing higher payments than originally negotiated. But you can also make lump-sum payments to reduce the loan size before maturity.

Charlton says paying off a loan can be viewed in the same way as setting aside a monthly sum for savings purposes or making a regular monthly mutual fund contribution with an automatic deduction from your bank account — something many financial planners recommend. Instead of automatically saving $200 or $300 a month, you can use the same money as a loan payment. The key is to borrow only an amount that you can afford to carry in the long term and where your financial well-being will not be jeopardized if your investments don't work out as planned.

"The biggest impediment to borrowing is fear," Charlton says. "But people should allow intelligence to rule their behavior."

Investing, let alone borrowing to invest, is still a new idea to many Canadians who have traditionally let their savings sit in guaranteed annual investment certificates and who are tied to the sense of security of owning their own bricks and mortar.

But many older people who have homes are finding they can't live on the income currently provided by GICs. They haven't built up an adequate financial nest egg to pay their living costs and are forced into such unhappy alternatives as selling their homes or refinancing in the form of reverse mortgages.

"People don't bat an eye at borrowing for vacations, for a house or for a fridge, stove or furniture," Charlton says. "Canadians have taken on billions of dollars in credit card debt. They should open their eyes and see how borrowing can help secure their financial future."

There. I couldn't have said it better myself. (In fact, I did. Thank you, Ms. Hemeon.)

So, there you have them — the Five Laws of Wealth Creation. I believe in them so passionately, I want to repeat them all here:

1. Pay yourself first.
2. Set articulated financial goals.
3. Be a contrarian: Ignore the stock market and take the road less travelled.
4. Leverage human resources.
5. Leverage capital, by borrowing to invest.

I can think of no better way for people to guarantee that they will be able to smile happily and securely, when they are confronted by the 65- or 70-year-old people who dwell within them.

So much for laws. Now, what about the Three Amazing Ts?

10

Wealth Creation and the Amazing Ts

EVERY schoolchild has heard of — but hardly any of them understands — Albert Einstein's famous equation of $E = mc^2$ (Energy equals Mass multiplied by the speed of light squared). However, few people know, and most certainly do not understand, the following equation, which will never win me any Nobel Prize, but is guaranteed to make every reader of this book a lot of money over the next few decades, if he or she will only heed it:

$$WC = T + T + T$$

Before you break into the same sweat that you did when confronting chemistry exams back in high school, let me quickly translate this for you: Wealth Creation equals the three Ts, or benefits, of compounding: Time, Total Rate of Return, and Taxation.

Now, what do I mean by each of these precious, wealth-creating Ts?

The Power of the First T: Time

The best way I can capture the incredible power and glory of compound interest in creating wealth is by recalling one of the great myths of the American people: the sale of the island of Manhattan by the native people who lived there in the early 17th century for (purportedly) $24 worth of trinkets.

Whether or not this actually happened, let's use this seemingly "bad real estate deal" to illustrate my point. Had these Native Americans taken that money offered to them by the Dutch settlers in cash, and invested it at 8% annually at a bank, that $24 — around 375 years later — would be worth a total of $50,000,000,000,000. You read right: 50 trillion dollars.

To put that amount in a bit of perspective, let us note that the national debt of the United States today is around $3 trillion. And the total amount of publicly traded securities on all the stock market exchanges of the United States is only around $1.5 trillion.

So, with the $50 trillion earned from that original $24, the descendants of the those early real-estate-selling Native Americans could purchase not just the island of Manhattan, but the entire country, many times over.

Obviously, three-plus centuries is a long period of time, but the point is still relevant. Interest compounded year after year after year can lead to some pretty astonishing amounts if left alone. The benefits of compounding can be truly amazing, when they are given time to work.

The Power of the Second T: Total Rate of Return

When we wish to look at the second of our three Ts, all of them necessary for wealth creation, let's continue our analogy of the Native Americans who sold Manhattan for so very little money.

Let us say that those Indians could not find a bank that would provide them with 8% annual interest, and they had to settle for only 6% on their $24 investment, back in 1626. You may be stunned to discover that, over the same period of nearly 375 years, when that tiny amount was invested at 6% compounded annually, their descendants would now discover that their great inheritance was $50 billion dollars.

Now, $50 billion is not a paltry sum, but please realize my key point here: By investing at a rate of only 2% less than they had hoped — 6% compounded annually, rather than the first example of 8% compounded annually — our Indian friends would eventually end up with only *one thousandth of the value of our first example.*

Think about it: $50 trillion, down to $50 billion, because of a lousy 2-percent-lower interest rate. What better example of the power of *total rate of return* could we possibly have than that?

The Power of the Third T: Taxation

When we look at taxation — that inescapable and always important part of life and, yes, of wealth creation — we shall leave our billionaire (or, if even luckier, trillionaire) Native Americans for a while, and turn to us, ourselves, today.

As I have declared elsewhere in this book, Revenue

Canada (or the Internal Revenue Service in the United States) is our partner in all of our investments. The question should be, How can we lessen their percentage of involvement in this unwilling partnership, and in a totally legal, acceptable fashion?

All investors are concerned about the capital gains tax that hits us all when we list various "gains" (from stocks, bonds, mutual funds, GICs, Canadian or U.S. Savings Bonds, etc.) in our annual income tax returns. But — and this is crucial — capital gains tax does not exist if you are a long-term buy-and-hold investor. Taxes are accruing, of course, but no taxes need be paid until the time when you choose to sell.

Conventional wisdom declares that "no one has ever gone broke taking a profit." I do not think that way. Why? Because there are huge advantages for an individual who chooses to get into a position where he or she makes but a few superior investments and then just sits back and watches them grow (over Time, our first T, and with an ever-growing Total Rate of Return, our second T), just like those very wealthy descendants of the Manhattan-dumping Native Americans in our earlier example. The advantages of buying and holding are endless:

- You will pay a lot fewer brokerage fees when you buy and hold.
- You will pay far fewer taxes to the government when you buy and hold.
- You can legally and happily delay paying any capital gains taxes indefinitely, through this wise strategy of not selling your investments continually.

- Through proper estate planning, your heirs will be able to inherit your estate with as little in taxes as possible on what you leave them.

To powerfully dramatize the benefits of that third T — taxation that is wisely deferred — imagine that you could invest one dollar every single year for 20 years and have it double over each of those years. (I must thank my mentor, Warren Buffett, for this inspired example.)

If you were in a 34% tax bracket, and you chose to sell your investment at the end of the first year, you would pay 34 cents in taxes on that one-dollar profit you made.

Now, of course, you are left with only $1.66 of your $2.00, to be reinvested, once again, at that attractive 100% annual return we discussed.

If you repeated this action every year for those two decades — sell your profit, pay the full capital gains tax, and then continue to reinvest the rest at that wonderful rate of 100% — you would have a gain of $25,200 at the end of the 20th year, after paying taxes of $13,000.

If, on the other hand, you purchased that same $1.00 investment that doubled each year, and chose not to sell it until the end of the 20th year, you would achieve a gain of $692,000, after paying taxes of approximately $356,000.

Therein lies the power of the Third T — taxation. By buying and holding, both you and the government of Canada have profited far more — no, wildly more — than if you had sold and bought every year over the two decades.

So What's That Formula Again?

$$WC = T + T + T$$

Wealth Creation equals (maximum) Time, plus (maximum) Total Return, plus (minimum) Taxation.

As you may have already surmised by now, everything that I have been sharing with you to this point in this section — from the wealthy Native Americans to the wealthy buy-and-holder who wisely avoids wasting his fortune in regular capital gains taxes — fits in perfectly with the (similarly simple) theories of my mentor, Warren Buffett. Which is why we now go . . .

Back to Buffett

You will recall from the earlier chapters and my Five Laws of Wealth Creation that multi-billionaire investor Warren Buffett invested not only in many publicly traded securities, but also in several businesses whose stock he came to own outright.

Indeed, over the past three decades, Mr. Buffett would often speak of his many investments in the wise and witty annual reports of his holding company, Berkshire Hathaway, and how interesting it was that he never differentiated between his passion for one (the ownership of minority interests in some companies) and the other (his 100% ownership of several other firms). To quote from his 1993 annual report, "An investor who owns a small piece of an outstanding business should hang on to it with the same tenacity as an individual who owned 100% of a company."

Walking his talk over the past year, Mr. Buffett purchased the remaining 49% of GEICO, the giant insurance company in which he had held 51% for so many years, and actually invested $1.5 billion in September 1996 to purchase all the shares of a major flight-simulator company — generously adding to the worth and value of every share of Berkshire Hathaway stock.

Let's not miss the major point I'm making above. Warren Buffett has not only held on to chunks of major companies (Coke, Gillette, Washington Post, World Book, several fine shoe companies, etc.) for many decades and never sold them, but he has actually avoided paying dividends to his many (happy) shareholders.

That may shock the majority of my readers. "But I have always been told to purchase stocks that pay dividends," you might say. "Don't the best stocks give out dividends when they have good years?"

But don't you see? By not paying out many millions of dollars of dividends to the shareholders of Berkshire Hathaway, and by plowing back into his company all those tens of millions of dollars in dividends his firm had been receiving (from Coke, Gillette, etc.) over the years, Mr. Buffett was able to build up massive amounts of money. And with that money, he was able to simply reach into the pot and purchase the remaining shares of GEICO and that huge flight-simulator company.

Warren Buffett would never have been able to buy those firms had he been paying out endless dividends to his share-holders. He simply kept reinvesting those dividends into his dozens of major companies.

The Foolishness of Jumping In and Out of the Stock Market

The vast majority of the public, and, unfortunately, of brokers and mutual fund managers, are continually preoccupied with the "lofty levels of the market," and, as a tragic result, are continuously trading in and out of the stock market, trying to achieve short-term gains.

This is one of the many investment "strategies" that involve forecasting and guesswork, and they are notoriously unreliable. I don't have to look very far to prove my point, and with great emphasis, too. Across the top of the Report on Business section of the *Globe and Mail* on Tuesday, November 12, 1996, ran the following headline: FUNDS MISS THE BOAT ON BANKS. The subheading of that (devastating, embarrassing) article explained their foolishness in greater detail: "Managers didn't own enough of hot sector to cash in on surge in prices."

Canadian bank stocks were suddenly hot. So hot, in fact, that even American investors and fund managers were buying in like crazy. The reason why they were so hot is obvious: Interest rates were down; people were eager to borrow more than ever before; mortgages were being taken out on homes in record numbers; profits from credit card debts skyrocketed (after all, there's lots of money to be made when you charge from 15% to 19% on people's credit cards while you're borrowing from the federal bank for only 4% or 5%). Each of Canada's major banks was announcing record profits — that's *profits*, not earnings — of a billion dollars and even more, every single quarter.

It should have been pretty obvious that bank stocks would soar.

The stock prices of Bank of Montreal, the Royal, Toronto Dominion, and the others actually shot up over 30% — a nearly one-third increase in value — between August 31, 1996, to a few days before the publication of that *Globe and Mail* article in mid-November of the same year.

Yet what did the geniuses at the various mutual funds — the so-called managers of your billions of dollars of investments, RRSPs, savings, etc. — decide to do? Why, they actually ignored these astonishing gains and chose not to purchase bank stocks for their mutual fund portfolios.

I found it interesting that one of the most successful mutual fund managers of the past several years was forced to mail out a newsletter to his tens of thousands of investors in which he admitted that he was "surprised by the strength of the financial services sector."

He was "surprised"! "Mortified" would have been a better choice of word. Here is what the same gentleman declared in an interview with the *Globe and Mail*, when investment reporter Andrew Bell asked him if he owned many bank stocks: "Nothing to speak of . . . We just missed them. Can't catch them all."

One wonders if some mutual funds "experts" could catch cold in a hospital influenza ward!

Here are some numbers to ponder, by both market "experts" and us. And they are no less powerful, even after the up-and-down year of 1999:

Between August 31, 1996, and November 8, 1996, financial stocks zoomed up over 30%, as noted above. Between those same 10 brief weeks, the entire Toronto Stock Exchange Index, which is made up of 300 stocks, shot up 12% (since banks and utilities account for nearly 17% of that indicator).

The shares of utilities were up over 15% during that minuscule period.

BCE Inc. of Montreal, once known as Bell Canada, leapt up 19%. Yet during those same few weeks (less than one-fifth of a year), here is how some of the most popular mutual funds did — because they ignored bank and utility stocks:

- Canadian Growth Fund increased 5.7%. (Not bad, for only a few weeks. But still . . .)
- Industrial Growth Fund and Industrial Horizon Fund both gained the same amount: 6.6%.
- Altamira Equity Fund, one of the most successful mutual funds of the past decade, rose 3.4%. (Oh, yes. That often-impressive fund actually fell 1.54% in September, before gaining that 3.4% in October and early November.)

Do you remember what I've said about "fear" in this book? Read this comment from a prominent money manager, as he explained why he wasn't buying bank stocks for his clients: "I'm nervous about the banks when you've got interest rates 2% lower than U.S. rates. That's artificial. That can't be sustained for a long period of time."

I'm so sorry that this gentleman was nervous about purchasing bank stocks, especially when they'd been announcing record earnings for over a year. But I'm even sorrier for his hundreds of thousands of clients, who lost out on far greater returns than they received — all because of this (usually) brilliant man's "fear."

Guess who didn't miss that dramatic run-up in the share prices of Canada's major banks in the fall of 1996? Investment managers such as Michael Lee-Chin of AIC, who is a buy-and-hold man in the great Buffett tradition. Mike sees himself as a "permanent shareholder" of the Bank of Montreal and the CIBC. Indeed, this same man, through his AIC Advantage Fund, has owned a large number of shares of a company called Fairfax Financial since the early 1980s. He purchased those shares at approximately $9 each. Today, including all the stock-splits and the reinvested dividends (remember my argument about not taking out dividends and having them taxed as capital gains, but rather leaving them in your portfolio?), each of those shares is currently valued (as of late 1999) at around $200 each — and they hit $600 in the late 1990s. Anyone care to bet against their hitting $600 again, early in the new millennium?

Now, imagine if Mr. Lee-Chin followed in the grand tradition of so many of the managers of great Canadian mutual funds who did not happen to have much faith in the financial sector of Canadian stocks in 1996. Would the extraordinary success story that is Fairfax Financial still be held tight and close in the AIC Advantage Fund portfolio today? I highly doubt it.

Businesses — Like Diamonds — Truly Are Forever

As I have noted so often throughout this book, the root of all wealth creation lies in business ownership. In every country of the world, the richest people are those who own businesses. (Once again, by "owning a business," I mean not only complete ownership but possessing common stocks of that business as well; do recall how Warren Buffett makes no distinction between the way he treats his "ownership" of less than one-tenth of the shares of Coca-Cola and the 100% he now owns of GEICO and several shoe and furniture companies. He loves and respects each company equally, and enjoys the great profits of each, by never touching their dividends and by never buying and selling the shares of either in a frivolous or panicky manner.)

But while the great value of business ownership may seem obvious, there is something that is too often less obvious, what I call the real value of a business, and sometimes its most important attribute. Surprisingly, this is overlooked by most people.

I suggest to you that the most important aspect of a business is its long-term ability to compound its earnings inside a "tax shelter" — in other words, the Three Ts that I discussed earlier. This is the astounding function of earnings, over time, without the negative effects of taxation.

This is a good place to give you a further example from the great Coca-Cola company. When that remarkable business first went public on the New York Stock Exchange in 1919, it cost a heady $40 a share. Sun Trust Bank of Atlanta was actually offered $100,000 in cash, in lieu of their underwriting fee, to get it on the exchange — or, if they preferred, they could be paid with a number of shares in the young company.

How wise they were to take the shares. Today, the common stock that Sun Trust chose to receive is valued in excess of $2.5 billion dollars. And this valuation is *not* because some manic-depressive stock market had artificially elevated those shares up to insane, lunatic levels. This skyrocketing value in Coca-Cola shares was simply the result of that company's ability to compound its value.

Warren Buffett once made a rather surprising declaration: "There is little difference between a business and a bond." How is that possible? Well, a bond will pay a fixed amount at a fixed rate for a certain period of time, correct? And a good business will do the same. But there is a very attractive difference between the two. Both bonds and businesses give income, but bonds have a fixed lifespan. Businesses can go on forever, and while their income can vary greatly (unlike a bond), they also have the potential of earning far greater percentages. And, best of all, a great and highly successful business can last for several generations, even indefinitely. Name a bond that can do that for you.

The great thing about both businesses and bonds is that magical Rule of 72, which many of you have read about, and which has actually been maligned as "the work of the devil" because it creates so much money with so little work. This quite lovely rule simply says that the length of time it takes for any investment to double in value is related to the number 72. So, for example:

- If the rate of compound interest available from a business or a bond is 12%, it will take 6 years for the principal to double in value (i.e., 12 times 6 is good old 72).
- If you are getting 9% on your investment, it will take 8 years for it to double in value.
- If you are getting 8% in interest, it will take 9 years for your initial sum to double, and so on.

Here is the thrill of compound interest in action. Which is why the Three Ts of Time, Total Return, and Taxation are so crucial to creating wealth. By taking his Time, continually reinvesting his Total Return, and never taking any money out, thus protecting it from Taxation, Warren Buffett was able to turn a company worth a few hundred thousand dollars into a multi-billion-dollar holding company in less than three decades.

I should note that many of my own clients, when they hear me follow this line of reasoning, become extremely agitated: "What do you mean I should never sell? How can I enjoy my wealth? I don't want to leave everything to the kids. I want to live a little, too!" The answer I give them is quite simple: By setting up a systematic withdrawal plan (see Chapter 13).

Let Us Pay Tribute to a Remarkable Woman

Remember our mythical billionaire/trillionaire Native Americans who invested the $24 that they foolishly accepted for Manhattan? Remember that their descendants today could have bought all of America several times over because of the magnificence of compound interest — the true value behind the great theory of the Three Ts?

That story was all about compound interest. But is compound interest really such a complex theory? Is the Rule of 72 actually as difficult to understand as Einstein's theory of relativity?

I don't think so. And to prove my point, let me refer to a glorious human being who was utterly unknown before the summer of 1995. It was then that this then 86-year-old African-American woman, Oseola McCarty, chose to donate nearly her entire savings — $150,000 — to pay for scholarships to the nearby University of Southern Mississippi.

You may well have heard of this woman over the past few years — especially when she passed away in the fall of 1999. After all, she was quickly written up on the front page of the *New York Times*, appeared on *Good Morning America*, was named one of the "10 Most Interesting People of 1995" by Barbara Walters, and much more. Why, the great jazz singer Roberta Flack sang to her, as did Patti LaBelle. President Clinton eagerly had his photo taken with her. Harvard gave her an honorary degree. Thousands of people have made pilgrimages to her tiny house in Hattiesburg, Mississippi, where she lived all of her life in a home bequeathed to her half a century ago by an uncle.

Now, why was the world so taken by this quiet, shy, modest, and deeply religious woman who dropped out of school when she was only eight years of age when she began to work as a laundress? Was it because she was so shockingly generous? Was it because this grade-school dropout, never-married woman, to quote the *New York Times* on November 12, 1996, "spent very little over the years, living so simply, amassing a small fortune a few one-dollar bills at a time"?

Yes, it was the latter that truly shocked us, and that's a shame. The sight of an elderly black woman giving away nearly every penny she ever earned, to offer scholarships to a southern American university is what really should move people.

But it is worth noting how Ms. McCarty saved so much money with so little investing. A book came out shortly before her death, entitled *Simple Wisdom for Rich Living*, filled with this old woman's down-home opinions on faith, work, clean living, and saving money.

I was struck by the brief entry on "savings": "The secret

to building a fortune is compounding interest." Ms. McCarty was a grand soul, and she ultimately knew more about financial planning than many of the millionaire, so-called "gurus" of the stock market about whom we've been reading for decades. She understood the power of "compounding interest" over time — so that taxation would not eat up her earnings — that allowed her to create college scholarships for generations to come.

The Three Ts work every time — and you don't need a Harvard MBA to understand the overwhelming power they possess. Just think of the late Miss Oseola McCarty of Hattiesburg, Mississippi.

But should your tastes run to the more educated, let me conclude with a remarkable statement made by the great scientist Albert Einstein when he was asked if the recently exploded atomic bomb, which grew out of his theories of energy and physics, had "just unleashed the most powerful force in the world." "No," the genius replied, "the most powerful force is compound interest."

11

Why Long-Term
Investments Are Best

THERE was a very funny cartoon carried in thousands of newspapers several years ago — it was from *Mother Goose and Grimm*, as I recall — and it struck me as a very fitting way to begin this passionately felt, cry-from-the-heart chapter.

Mother Goose has taken her cat to the vet. "Fetch!" the veterinarian yells at the cat.

The cat sits there.

"Jump!" the vet shouts.

The cat sits there.

"Roll over!" the vet orders.

The cat sits there.

Then the veterinarian turns to its owner and exclaims, "Your cat seems perfectly normal to me!"

The analogy quickly becomes clear. When your buddies, or your neighbours, or the business journalists, or even your broker all scream at you, "Sell!" (because of real or imagined problems in the stock market, panic, fears, or even a mini-crash), simply respond like that wise, healthy, and "perfectly normal" cat of Mother Goose: Just sit tight and wait it out. You will always come out on top, as I'll prove to you now with facts and statistics galore.

One could even play on the word "dog" here, since it's often used for a stock that goes down steadily, for it is dogs, not cats, that are often eager to "fetch," "jump," and "roll over." When you are truly invested in the stock market — and not merely gambling, by leaping in and out of your port-folio — then you must be clever, even lazy, like the wily cat, not wild and reckless like the eager-to-leap-at-your-bidding dog. Cats simply have no interest in listening to their own-ers; they just love to lie around and sleep away their lives. Which is what your excellent portfolio of fine "businesses" should be doing — year after year after year.

When I wrote an earlier version of this book in early 1997, the New York Stock Exchange had shot past the 7000 mark on the Dow Jones, followed closely behind by Canada's own Toronto Stock Exchange as it moved beyond 6000. And in the dying weeks of 1999, the two numbers were in the range of 11,000 and 7000, respectively. Naturally, this has a lot of people "worried" and "frightened" — and you already know my opinion about fear. Fear poverty, and you will surely be visited by it. What are some of these fears expressed almost daily by brokers, journalists, and analysts alike (and for the past several years in a row, by the way, as the stock markets of North America keep going up and up and up)?

- Dividends are too low.

- Stock prices are far too high.
- The mutual funds are buying too much, forcing those stock prices up artificially, and dangerously.

You may recall that I earlier described newspapers as the "Antichrists" of sensible investing. An example of what I spoke about blared out at me from a *USA Today* box in downtown Toronto a few years ago. It was the Tuesday, November 26, 1996, issue, and here are just a few "gems" I plucked from its cover story, entitled "Dauntless Dow: Too Far, Too Fast?"

With the Dow Jones Industrials setting record after record, posting a 28% gain this year on top of 1995's 33% gain, the notion of perpetually rising prices does not seem outrageous.

. . . As recently as Oct. 11, the Dow had never closed above 6,000. In November, the average has climbed 8.6%. That's the biggest monthly rise since December 1991 . . .

But instead of celebrating, professional money managers on Wall Street are worrying because the market has been making people so much money so fast.

If things don't cool off soon, the amazing stock boom could be followed by a sudden and dramatic bust or a painfully long bear market . . .

So good is the environment for stocks that some are likening it to nirvana. And there is talk that the stock market has entered a new age where century-old measures of value are no longer relevant.

All this scares market veterans. They know markets move from one extreme to another. The moves start with good reasons, but end after too much fear, or too much greed. They know that in bull markets investors move from using reason to conjuring up rationalizations for speculation . . .

Are these doomsayers right in their doomsaying? They will certainly be (eventually) correct in one sense: There *will* be a "correction" in the stock markets of this continent, and probably around the world, over the next month/year/years; indeed, there have been several "corrections" during 1999.

How do I know? Because history tells me so. There are clear patterns in the behaviour of stock markets, just as there are in the rest of life. If you tell me that it has snowed in your city before December 1 every other year for a century, I think it's a pretty fair assumption that it'll snow before that date this year — or next. And if you've suffered from hay fever nearly every summer since you were a teenager, the chances are good that . . . (you see what I'm getting at).

Here's a fact for you, and I hope you won't let it fill you with fear. Since 1900, stocks on the New York Stock Exchange have *declined* by at least 10%, and sometimes more than that, on over 50 separate occasions. That's an average of slightly more than one "major correction" every two years or so, throughout this century.

Here's another fact. On fully 15 of those 50+ corrections in the marketplace, stocks have gone down a full one-quarter of their price, and even more.

To put this another way, approximately every half-dozen years the stock exchanges of North America experience some severe — if rarely long-lasting — setbacks.

Now, how should one react to these relatively frequent, if unpleasant, occurrences in the stock market? Most people, sadly, tend to respond to any so-called bear market with panic selling, loss of faith in the stocks they are holding, disappointment with their broker, fears for their financial future. Yet the patterns of stock market corrections are there and should surprise nobody.

As a parent, I cannot resist an analogy: If we screamed "I give up" and threw our children bodily out of the house every time they talked back to us, disobeyed us, broke curfew, smoked behind our backs, or skipped school, our streets would be so filled with homeless youth that we wouldn't be able to move from store to store.

Yet that is precisely how the majority of "investors" acts when the stock markets go through those periodic, almost regular, corrections. "Sell everything!" we scream at our brokers. "I've had it with gambling!" "And I'm firing you, too!"

Stop Speculating — and Really, Truly Invest

Well, I've had it with speculating, too. Which is why I purchase only quality companies for my clients, since I recognize that in every correction, all companies (whether they are good, bad, or indifferent) see their stock prices decline. Please recall the major correction in the last decade that I mentioned earlier in this book, that pushed Warren Buffett's amazing Berkshire Hathaway holding company down from $8900 a share to less than $6000. That's a brutal drop. But it didn't take long for wise investors to recognize that Berkshire continued to hold billions of dollars in Coke, Gillette, and dozens of other great businesses, and had lost none of its inherent value. So what happened? Its stock price quickly rose far beyond its earlier high, to over $33,000 in late 1996.

As I now write, it is in the $60,000 range. True, it hit $80,000 in 1998, but if you had purchased Berkshire Hathaway at $6000 — or even at the $30,000 it was at when I wrote an earlier version of this book — would you be complaining? Those are corrections most of us would welcome.

Yet these nearly inevitable "corrections" continue to freak out, depress, and terrify investors every single time. And people respond by doing absolutely destructive things to their portfolios. They "hedge their bets" (as if long-term investing in solid businesses can ever be labelled "betting") by playing far riskier games in the market, such as "shorting" on stocks (selling shares before you actually own them, while hoping that they will fall in value before you have to pay up). Or they buy options or futures, practices I refuse to even discuss in this book. This is all speculative behaviour.

The other foolish thing that far too many "investors" do when these corrections occur is sell off large amounts of various stocks and mutual funds, and then sit on their diminished money, hoping that prices will fall lower and lower — but (naturally) they are never quite sure when they should "climb back in." And who can be sure? Indeed, most of the truly successful investors of our time, from John Templeton (founder of the Templeton mutual funds) to Peter Lynch (former fund manager at Fidelity Investments) to my own mentor Warren Buffett, are forever preaching how futile it is to attempt to guess which direction the markets are going to head — and when they will head there.

I have noted throughout this book, and it's worth mentioning again, that corrections in the market are the best time to purchase quality firms at a good price.

I could give you thousands of statistics of solid companies that have been battered during the several dozen corrections of the past century, and prove to you how they always come back stronger than ever, like a good prizefighter who gets knocked down briefly and climbs up again. Following are a few quite striking examples of some great American stocks over the past quarter century.

Banc One Corp. hit a low of $1.60 in 1974, after having reached $2.87 a share the year before. During that "crash" of 1987 that everyone still talks about with horror, its stock crumbled to $9.70 after peaking at $16.12 the same year. At the turn of the century, as I write this book, one share of Banc One will cost you over $35.

Is that "recovery" enough for you? No? Then how about this example. The common stock of Disney hit a low of 97 cents during the correction of 1973-74, after reaching a high of $6.89. During 1987, its stock fell from $20.63 to $10.31. Today, Disney shares go for $25. (Maybe I should mention that Disney underwent a three-for-one split in the fall of 1998.)

Since most of us enjoy eating hamburgers almost as much as visiting Disney World, let's look at McDonald's shares over those same periods. In 1973-74, that great company's shares veered between $3.80 and $1.05; in 1987, the range was $15.28 and $7.84. Today? Over $43 a share. And the company went through a two-for-one split in early 1999. And lest you think that Warren Buffett is some kind of god and never makes mistakes (and always follows his own advice), let me quote from his always witty annual report, this one from 1998: ". . . my decision to sell McDonald's was a very big mistake."

Procter & Gamble is another company whose products we use frequently, even daily. How did its shares do in each of those periods? Back in the early '70s, P&G common stock ranged between $8.38 and $15; in that scary crash of 1987 it slumped from a high of $42.44 to a low of $15. In late 1999, you had to pay over $98 for a single share.

And we mustn't ignore those two favourite companies of Warren Buffett of Berkshire Hathaway. Coca-Cola and Gillette both show similar successes, after similar roller-coaster rides. The soft drink stock ranged between $1.86 and $6.25 in '73-'74; in 1987, between $7.00 and $13.28; today, it's selling for over $53 a share — after a two-for-one split, of course.

And Gillette? The early 1970s saw it drop from $4.13 to $1.30; 1987 witnessed a crumbling from $11.47 down to $4.41. Today? Big surprise. In the fall of 1999, one share is worth over $38. (It split two-for-one back in the summer of 1998.)

And you wondered why Warren Buffett is one of the wealthiest men in America? And maybe you still wonder, as well, why you — and millions of others — panic needlessly every time the stock markets of the world undergo those fairly regular "corrections." As Peter Lynch, the great investor, once noted about the chairman of Berkshire Hathaway's billion-dollar personal fortune, "He got there by picking stocks and not by switching in and out of them."

What's Gained — and Lost — by Jumping In and Out of the Market

Stocks — like sports teams and the careers of movie stars — have their good and bad years, and the stock markets of the world have good and bad months. Here are some choice comments from Peter Lynch, which I found in both speeches and print over the past few years:

People who exit the stock market to avoid a decline are odds-on favorites to miss the next rally. If you don't believe corporate profits will continue to rise, and you can't stomach a decline in the market, don't buy stocks or equity mutual funds.

If you were out of stocks in 40 key months over the past 40 years, your annual return on investment dropped from 11.4% to 2.7%. You underperformed your savings account.

Since 1965, if you bought stocks once a year and were unlucky enough to pick the worst day to invest (when stocks were at their highest prices) 30 years in a row, you ended up with an annual return of 10.6%. If you were incredibly lucky and invested on the best day of the year 30 years in a row, you ended up with an annual return of 11.7%. So the difference between perfect timing and horrendous timing is 1.1%. This timing business is much ado about very little.

Stocks outperformed bonds in eight out of the nine previous decades in this century, and they are well ahead halfway through this one [the 1990s].

As Warren Buffett, Peter Lynch, and I would all put it: Stick around and don't bail out when those relatively regular "corrections" happen. And if you do panic, remember Mr. Lynch's numbers, and some of the stock price swings of Disney, McDonald's, Coke, and Gillette and dozens of other quality, innovative, ever-growing companies over the past quarter century; those numbers should certainly give you strength to carry on and "hold on" — as the most successful investors do.

But Why Risk Playing the Stock Market at All?

The above is a perfectly legitimate question many millions of North Americans ask themselves, and which, unfortunately, a good percentage of them choose to answer in the negative.

So what do they do instead? They "play it safe," by tip-toeing gently into the very safe (and very predictable, and exceedingly unprofitable) world of GICs, treasury bills, and bonds. The people who are most guilty of this are those who are retired or over 65, and who fear that, with no more money coming in from their jobs, they'd better avoid "those dangerous up-and-down stocks."

Wrong, wrong, wrong. And to prove my point, I turn to a quite fascinating study by three finance professors at York University in Toronto, who put together a very impressive study which suggested that — and I here quote the *Globe and Mail* article on the professors, Kwok Ho, Moshe Arye Milevsky, and Chris Robinson — "holding substantial equities [stocks] in retirement actually increases long-term safety."

In other words, seniors who buy and hold stocks not only will live in far better style in their later years but will actually minimize the horror of so many older people, that they might outlive their savings. (Think of what happened to that tragic couple in their 80s who came to my office in the fall of 1996, whom I described earlier in this book.)

What the professors discovered deserves stressing here. Equity investments — stocks — outperform fixed-income ones, such as GICs, CSBs, and U.S. Savings Bonds, by a wide margin.

Professor Robinson of York quotes from Statistics Canada "mortality tables," and although they are very hopeful for those of us who wish to live long lives, the same tables can be extremely discomforting for those of us who have not thoughtfully planned financially for the future. A woman who has made it to the age of 65 today has a 50% chance of living to the age of 85, a 31% chance of making it to 90, and a 12% chance of living to the age of 95.

And what about today's 65-year-old man? He has a 28% chance of living to 85, a 15% chance of making it to 90, a 4% chance of living to 95.

When the good professors of York University looked at those statistics, they concluded, "If you want to choose a planning horizon, it should be at least 95 for a woman and 90 for a man."

Now, that's all well and good, if you've got a million bucks socked away, and how many of us have been fortunate enough to achieve that? But notice what these scholars discovered, using a relatively familiar situation. A 65-year-old woman retires with $560,000 in savings and wishes to have, say, $40,000 each year in inflation-indexed income. (This means that, because of inflation, the $40,000 she needed in the first year after leaving the workforce will turn into $42,000 in the second year, and then more and more and more as time goes on.)

Here's the horror story. That cautious 65-year-old woman who invested her money in, say, treasury bills, will have a 65% chance of outliving her capital. But if she took the same money and invested 95% of it (or more) into quality common stocks, that horrific probability of running out of money falls to only 28%.

Even the average man, with his traditionally shorter life-span, encounters a similarly scary ride with those so-called safe and prudent investments. In the same situation, a 65-year-old man will still have a 45% probability of outliving his accumulated capital with all of his money in T-bills. Yet this probability falls to a mere 19% if he holds 90% or more of his savings in equities.

The way these three York professors reached the above conclusions is very interesting. They noted that in the 43 years between 1950 and 1993, the average annual (after-inflation) return on 91-day Canadian treasury bills was a mere 1.5%. Government of Canada long-term bonds produced a return that was little better: a measly 2.8%. Yet over the exact same period, the Toronto Stock Exchange 300 Composite Index returned an average of 7.7%. The man and woman I've been describing could have retired with millions if they had chosen to buy quality stocks in excellent businesses, whether in Canada or the United States, and would never even have come close to finding themselves "outliving their capital."

The York University professors give many other examples in their study, but the point they make should already be both clear and vital. Even with those sometimes nerve-wracking fluctuations that I've been describing in this chapter as "corrections" (for T-bills, the variance has averaged a mere 3.9%, for bonds, 10.4%, for stocks, 17.2%), to quote Professor Robinson, "equities remain crucial, because of their higher long-term returns."

Which is why I continue to stress throughout this book that you should buy quality businesses, or parts of good businesses (as represented by their common shares listed on public exchanges), and hold them for long lengths of time while continually reinvesting any dividends. The result will invariably be a happy, worry-free retirement. The men and women who continually turn to GICs, treasury bills, and bonds are the true risk-takers in the world of investing, *not* those who choose to "play" the market. Cash was never intended to be a storehouse of value, and it should not be used that way.

After one of their many victories over far more numerous and well-armed enemies, the Israelis were once asked why they kept winning, and they answered with an interesting expression: "Ayn B'rayra" — "There is no alternative." It was a powerful declaration. The Arabs can lose a battle and still have their countries, their leaders, their nations, the Israelis explained. But if we lose even once, we would be doomed and have nothing to fall back on. With all due respect, I think the phrase "there is no alternative" could be applied to anyone who feels that he or she can rely on GICs or Canada Savings Bonds: There is no alternative to careful, thoughtful, wise, long-term investing.

As I said at the opening of this chapter, be a cat in the world of equities, and not a dog. Don't jump, fetch, or leap for anyone — even in response to the largest correction in the market. Just curl up and sleep, on a soft, warm blanket of good common shares of excellent businesses and quality mutual funds. And avoid the "safe" world of GICs, treasury bills, and bonds as you would the plague.

12

Buy Mutuals —
but Buy Their Stocks

As a man who has made a fine living over the past two decades by recommending mutual funds to my clients, I am not about to bad-mouth that admirable investment vehicle. Indeed, since the fund I co-founded back in the mid-80s, AIC, has seen its Advantage mutual fund shoot up from an initial offering of $5.00 to around $60 at the time of writing, I am well aware of just how wonderfully mutual funds can grow for their investors. Especially when they are run by people who firmly believe in the principles I've been stressing throughout this book. And which I am doing today with the new family of Dynamic Infinity mutual funds.

But I'm now about to make a declaration that may seem surprising, but it sure won't be so shocking once I give you the facts and figures. Here goes: There is no mutual fund that can grow as rapidly or as successfully as a publicly traded mutual fund company.

Think about this for a few moments, please.

Any mutual fund — no matter how excellent its managers, no matter how wise and thoughtful (and lucky) its owners — must invest in many different stocks and bonds. That is their mandate, and many do it with brilliance.

But think about the mutual fund industry, if you will. It is the joyful recipient of an astounding, astonishing boom, which goes back over a quarter century. In 1977, just over twenty years ago, the total amount of money invested in mutual funds across North America was approximately $50 billion, which seemed impressive at the time.

Today, that number is in excess of $5 trillion! Indeed, there are now more mutual funds available than there are stocks listed on the New York Stock Exchange.

Let's look at Canada alone. When I first joined the field in 1979, less than $1 billion was invested in mutual funds by our fellow countrymen. Ten years later, it was perhaps $5 billion. Today, at the beginning of a new century, that sum is shooting past $430 billion.

The Times, They Really Are a-Changin'

Scholars like to describe poets and artists as the "antennae" of society, and in many ways they are. Oftentimes, great writers and artists suggest, even predict, massive changes about to affect society, long before economists, professors, and politicians. But the occasional businessman can also have very acute antennae, as well. I think of Henry Ford, who was hardly the first person to "invent" the automobile, but he was, inarguably, the genius who created the assembly line, which eventually put North America, and the entire world, on wheels. Ford did something else that was just as inspired. He offered "five dollars a day" as wages in the early 1930s, at a time when the vast majority of other businesses were paying their employees only a dime, maybe a quarter, an hour. "He's crazy!" exclaimed most of America's politicians and economists. "He'll go broke!"

Henry Ford thought otherwise, and we know now who was correct. He had figured out that if he gave his employees high enough wages, they would be better able to purchase the automobiles they were assembling.

Ford was a visionary, and his antennae were certainly amazing. But it doesn't take a visionary to see massive changes ahead based on the massive changes that have been occurring for several decades in the saving and investing habits of North Americans.

We are presently going through one of the most powerful demographic shifts in history, across North America and around the world. As the tens of millions of so-called Baby Boomers edge into their 50s and prepare for their respective retirements, they are no longer convinced (as their parents had been) that their governments will have the ability (much less the philosophy or even desire) to fund their retirement and health through social service programs and the so-called safety net.

One does not even have to read the daily paper to make note of the slashing away at various programs by Ottawa, and in more and more provinces, from Alberta to Ontario and beyond. Not only are there massive deficits on both federal and provincial levels, but the one or two retired people of today who have nearly a half-dozen other working Canadians paying into the Canada Pension Plan for them will soon change to a half-dozen people in retirement for every one person still on a payroll. Worker-to-retiree percentages are similarly scary in the United States as we move into the new millennium.

Is it any wonder that mutual funds have become an attractive investment? And, here is what is most relevant to this chapter, as well as to the theme of this book: Mutual fund companies — several of which have publicly traded stocks on exchanges around the world — fall into that same category I've been stressing throughout this text. They are superior businesses that are in strong, long-term growth industries. And if they are run with honest, careful, share-holder-managers, they will create great value.

But here is where mutual fund stocks differ from, say, minor soft drink companies or merely competent computer businesses. Even mediocre mutual fund company stocks are good investments, because of this extraordinary momentum, this hurricane-like wind in the sales of the mutual fund industry.

I wish I could claim some kind of epiphany like the Bible's Saul of Tarsus purportedly had on the road to Damascus, when I suddenly woke up to the phenomenal potential — and actual growth — in the stocks of mutual fund compa-nies. Alas, it was far more prosaic; indeed, it took several years to sink in. Here's what happened. Back in the 1981 recession, when I was in my third year of selling mutual funds, I found the resistance of buyers to be exceedingly high. High? The CN Tower of Toronto and Chicago's Sears Tower would look like two-storey buildings in comparison. My good friend Michael Lee-Chin and I, as I noted above back in Chapter 1, had been selling mutual funds for one of the great mutual fund sales firms of Canada, Regal Capital Planners, in the Hamilton, Ontario, area, and the winter was bleak. And I don't mean just the weather.

Interest rates were up to a usurious 21% — meaning that people were not too eager to invest in mutual funds, or anything else, for that matter; there was simply too much competition for their inflation-battered money. Indeed, Canada Savings Bonds were offering a stunning 19% that same year, also putting the mutual fund industry in the shade, if not leaving it in the dust.

It was punishingly difficult to make any mutual fund sale. It got so bad, I was seriously considering a return to the insurance business, which I had left with some relief only a few years earlier. And Michael was even thinking of returning to his home and native land of Jamaica.

Around this same time, Mackenzie, one of the largest mutual fund companies in Canada, decided to move from its humble beginnings over a fish-and-chips shop, where it shared premises with one of its benefactors at Cara Foods. So Michael and I visited their snazzy new offices at 150 Bloor Street West in Toronto.

We were both dazzled by what we saw. Who could these people be? Beautiful china! Impressive hors d'oeuvres! Magnificent wood paneling! These people must have been printing money, while Michael and I were struggling to make ends meet.

In retrospect, they were printing money, and there was good reason why we salesmen were not doing very well. We had the added burdens of maintaining staff, having client services in place, and encountering significant buyer resistance to mutual fund sales. As Bob Dylan wittily sang, some years earlier, " . . . something is happening here / But you don't know what it is / Do you, Mister Jones?"

We didn't know, even then. It took Michael and me another year or two before it finally hit home: A mutual fund company is a fantastic, reliable, trustworthy investment. My friend was struck by the potential of the common stock of Mackenzie Financial, which was then selling in the range of 50 to 60 cents on the Toronto Stock Exchange. So he went ahead and arranged a loan (remember my Fifth Law of Wealth Creation — borrow to invest) and invested heavily in the common shares of Mackenzie.

I almost hate to think about what his original investment is worth today, because knowing Michael Lee-Chin, whose philosophy is the same as mine and Warren Buffett's, he probably never sold it. Mackenzie common stock has gone from strength to strength (to strength) ever since, as you'll see below.

Another Writer's Thoughts about the Greatness of Mutual Fund Companies' Stocks

I've been confessing how slow I was to recognize the spectacular growth in the very industry in which I laboured. Thank heavens I wasn't alone in this blindness. (How many people saw the explosion in the number of cars on the streets and highways of North America back in the 1910s and 1920s, and promptly opened gas stations or tire companies or repair shops?)

Peter Lynch, labelled "#1 money manager" by *Time* magazine, made a rather mortifying confession in his 1989 best-seller, *One Up on Wall Street*:

Who could have had a greater advantage than yours truly, sitting in an office at Fidelity during the boom in financial services and in the mutual funds? . . .

I'd been coming to work here for nearly two decades. I know half the officers in the major financial-service companies. I follow the daily ups and downs, and I could notice important trends months before the analysts on Wall Street. You couldn't have been more strategically placed to cash in on the bonanza of the early 1980s. [Author's Note: The bonanza continues, nearly two decades later, and it will not stop for many years to come, if ever.]

The people who print prospectuses must have seen it — they could hardly keep up with all the new shareholders in the mutual funds. The sales force must have seen it as they crisscrossed the country in their Winnebagos and returned with billions in new assets. The maintenance services must have seen the expansion in the offices at Federated, Franklin, Dreyfus, and Fidelity. The companies that sold mutual funds prospered as never before in their history. The mad rush was on.

Fidelity isn't a public company, so you couldn't invest in the rush here. But what about Dreyfus? Want to see a chart that doesn't stop? The stock sold for 40 cents a share in 1977, then nearly $40 a share in 1986, a 100-bagger in nine years, and much of that during a lousy stock market. Franklin was a 138-bagger, and Federated was up 50-fold before it was bought out by Aetna. I was right on top of all of them. I knew the Dreyfus story, the Franklin story, and the Federated story from beginning to end. Everything was right, earnings were up, the momentum was obvious . . .

How much did I make from all this? Zippo. I didn't buy

a single share of any of the financial services companies: not Dreyfus, not Federated, not Franklin. I missed the whole deal and didn't realize it until it was too late . . . [Note: It's still not too late; see below.]

In his follow-up volume in 1993, *Beating the Street*, Lynch admitted once again how he (seemingly, but not really) "missed the boat" on the explosive growth of mutual fund company stocks. Then he added an interesting comment, well worth repeating here, because it emphasizes one of my major themes in this book: Corrections, those regular dips in the stock market, should be seen as fabulous opportunities to pick up stocks at bargain prices.

After noting the "fear of the collapse of the mutual-fund industry after the Great Correction of 1987," Lynch declared:

> That correction gave me the chance to buy these fellow mutual-fund companies, which I had overlooked before, and at low prices. Here is another of my favorite what-if portfolios: If you had divided your money equally among these . . . stocks [Dreyfus, Franklin Resources, Colonial Group, T. Rowe Price, State Street Bank, Alliance Capital Management, and Eaton Vance] and held them from the beginning of 1988 to the end of 1989, you would have out-performed 99 percent of the funds that these companies promote.

Thinking about Peter Lynch and quoting from his two books makes me think of another major point I wish to make. Lynch's boss at Fidelity, Ned Johnson, is among the top 10 richest people in America, because he owns 100% of that company. (He chose his father well, and inherited it; we should all have such problems.) As Lynch noted in his books, Fidelity is not public, so the only person who truly benefitted from it is that one man, Ned Johnson, whose family firm manages over $825 billion in mutual funds today around the world, over $22 billion in Canada alone.

But isn't it informative that the brilliant, creative stock-wheeler-and-dealer Peter Lynch, who was Fidelity's most famous manager for many years, has never come close to being in the Forbes Four Hundred richest people? Sure, he's worth tens of millions of dollars; he's invested well, and he's had two best-selling business books. But Ned Johnson, his long-time boss at Fidelity, whom we hear of far less frequently than his most successful trader, is worth many billions of dollars — or over 1000 times the fortune of Peter Lynch.

You already know why Johnson is wealthier than Lynch; he owns a mutual fund company. And if you choose to (wisely) buy into a major mutual fund company's publicly traded stock, you will own a mutual fund company, too, just like Ned Johnson. Or at least a tiny piece of one. And, as noted above, mutual fund companies have the wind in their sails, and that wind will probably never stop blowing. After all, because of the shift from spending to saving among a growing number of aging Canadians, some predict that the mutual fund industry in Canada will have over one trillion dollars invested in its products by the year 2005.

Why Mutual Fund Company Stocks
Are the Way to Go

I've already suggested that there has been a tremendous demographic shift in North America, thanks to the tens and tens of millions of "babies" born to servicemen returning from the Second World War, who are now all edging into their 50s and have money to invest in the "safety" and "security" of mutual funds.

But there is another reason why mutual fund companies are such fabulous investment possibilities. Let me make a few analogies to prove my point.

If you run a bakery or a fruit store, you've got to worry about your products going stale or rotten before you sell them. If you run a publishing company, you must be concerned with books that don't sell, advances against royalties that never get earned out, contracts that never get fulfilled, writers' blocks, lack of government grants, and more. If you run an oil company, you must worry about tensions in the Middle East, Arab boycotts, government taxation, reserves, and so on.

But if you run a mutual fund company — or own a common stock of one — you own a continuous revenue stream that flows from total assets under administration. No bread going stale or fruit going bad or books remaindered or oil shortages in the financial industry. No factories to heat, no tools to break down, no accounts receivable, no shipping, no handling, no warehousing. It is, quite literally, a perpetual money machine.

Here is something else that is quite interesting. Software companies who do not market well or keep inventing new and more creative products will go down the tube. The same with dress shops or restaurants that don't keep up with fashion, or advertise well, or treat their customers with respect.

Yet this is precisely where mutual fund companies also differ, and substantially so, from nearly every other kind of business or service industry. Even if a mutual fund practises asset allocation (which is not a favourite of mine), it will do well. Or uses sector rotation (another non-favourite). Or leaps in and out of the market like a Mexican jumping bean (which I abhor). Indeed, even if the money manager of a mutual fund has his own, twisted interpretation of a "long-term hold" on stocks as being "a maximum of two weeks," it will thrive. Even if it holds cash for too long, or emerging securities that never quite emerge enough, or buys bonds — all of which I disdain — it will go from strength to strength to strength.

Why? Because management fees are generated on a continuous basis for any fund management company. Because every single mutual fund share sold — and there are billions of them — brings a little more money into the firm that handles it. So, when you own shares of a mutual fund company, your revenue continually streams in from every single mutual fund they manage — no matter how questionably they choose to manage it. Owning the mutual fund company is where it's at, not the mutual fund.

The above is only partially true, of course. Mutual funds are an essential part of every financial portfolio, and I don't mean "asset allocation" here. Mutual funds may rise less than mutual fund company stocks and other great, growth industries, but they also do not fall as far in those trying times of correction. So, for "smoothing out the edges," I always recommend mutual funds — especially ones such as the Infinity family of funds, which I co-launched in early 1997 and which is now part of the Dynamic Mutual Fund family, owned by Dundee Bancorp. Infinity invests "the Warren Buffett way," in quality businesses, and, yes, in mutual fund company shares.

Everything I am sharing with you here is public knowledge. But let's talk international mutual fund companies for a moment. Peter Lynch referred to Dreyfus zooming up a hundred-fold in just a few years. But look at these others, from both the U.S. and around the world.

- T. Rowe Price went public in 1980, when it was managing some $20 million in its mutual funds; today, it handles over $70 billion of other people's money. So what happened to its stock on the NYSE? It grew by over 1000% over the past decade. (Does that company handle a mutual fund that has gone up by 200%, much less five times that? Of course not — which is the point of this chapter.)
- Perpetual Asset Management of Great Britain went public much later. If you had invested $10,000 in 1991, its best-managed mutual fund would be worth just over $25,000. But the same money invested in Perpetual Asset Management common stock would be worth over $500,000 in less than a decade.

But who has to go around the world, changing your Canadian dollars into American bucks or British pounds? Let's look at our own beloved country.

- AGF Management Limited is a fine Canadian mutual fund company, and you certainly would have done well investing $10,000 in its AGF American Growth Class mutual fund in 1984, worth $62,236 in 1999, if all income and dividends were taken. But if all dividends were reinvested, that $10,000 would have been worth $91,442 in those 15 years. Ah, but if you had invested that same amount of $10,000 in its publicly traded management company, AGF stock, on the TSE, your $10,000 nest egg would have hit $242,941, if you kept all dividends, and $426,080, if all dividends had been reinvested.

- How about $10,000 invested in Trimark's Canadian Fund mutual fund in 1981? It was worth over $89,000 as of June 1999. The same amount in its Trimark Fund in 1981? Over $171,000 as of the summer of 1999. But if you had invested in Trimark's stock on the TSE, at its initial $12 offering, your investment would have been worth nearly $100 per share at the turn of the century.

- And what of Mackenzie Financial Corporation, whose new offices so "wowed" Michael Lee-Chin and me back in the early 1980s? Ten thousand dollars invested in January 1968 in their Industrial Growth Fund was worth nearly five times as much 10 years later, over $230,000 two decades after that, and, in January 1999 that original $10,000 was worth an astonishing $489,686.50, just 31 years after the original investment. It would have been a superb investment. But $10,000 invested in Mackenzie Financial Corporation stock, at the launch of its public company in the fall of 1981, was worth just over $1 million on September 30, 1999 (assuming all

dividends were reinvested). Ten thousand dollars to
$1 million in just over 18 years!

- I wish to add Dundee Bancorp here, and not only
  because I have recently joined this great firm, but
  because it fits into the theories I am suggesting
  throughout this chapter. If you put $10,000 into (what
  is now called) Dynamic Power Canadian Growth Fund
  in 1989, it would be worth $33,000 today, in late 1999.
  This is a 12.6% average annual compounded rate of
  growth, and a lot better than you would have gotten
  in any bank account, CSB, or GIC. But note this. When
  Dundee Bancorp went public in 1992, it came out at
  $3.00, quickly dropped to $2.00 ("Sell, sell, sell!" I'm
  sure that all the brokers screamed), and then shot up
  to $43 in the fall of September 1998. And while it is
  well below that high at the end of 1999 (it's in the $15
  range), it is still up 500% from its original price in less
  than eight years. Pretty good, eh? And in the fall of
  1999, a new stock was listed on the TSE — Dundee
  Wealth Management Inc., of which 85% was owned by
  Dundee Bancorp. Care to guess how a new financial
  stock such as this one will do in the next decade or
  two? Take a look at AGF and Mackenzie and Trimark's
  respective stocks, and you'll get some ideas.

Over my many years working with Michael Lee-Chin to
build AIC into a real force and huge success in the mutual
fund field, I have often been asked why its funds have done
so spectacularly well. After all, many mutual funds are successful one year but below par the next; only a few make it
into the top 10, year after year after year.

Well, people like to say that ideas are "a dime a dozen," but as far as I'm concerned it's the man or woman who implements those ideas who has the real value. Indeed, he or she is priceless. The visionary responsible for the amazing growth of the AIC Advantage Fund, Michael Lee-Chin, saw this phenomenal opportunity in the mutual fund industry itself — at the same time that Peter Lynch, the "genius" of Fidelity, down on Wall Street, did not. Michael asked himself, In what way can my clients better participate in the growth of this wonderful industry than by owning shares of publicly traded mutual fund companies?

And so, Michael made sure that AIC Advantage Fund became a significant shareholder in Mackenzie's stock, and later, AGF's, and ultimately those of Trimark and Dundee and CI Fund Management and Investors Group.

It was an irresistible combination of two inspired concepts: buying excellent businesses and holding them "forever," à la Warren Buffett, and recognizing that mutual fund companies are among the greatest money-manufacturers in human history.

I hope that I've explained the theory clearly — no, really a rule — that I proposed at the start of this chapter. Mutual fund companies, through their publicly traded common shares, are an essential part of any successful portfolio. Of course, people should also own individual mutual funds (I heartily recommend the new Infinity family, of which I am the chief portfolio strategist), since they invariably help "smooth out the bumps."

I cannot stress enough what a fantastic future lies in store for the mutual fund industry, and the stocks of the major mutual fund companies don't accurately track what's happening out there. Analysts like Mark Maxwell have pointed out how the world of mutual funds will grow at ever-increasing levels, relative to other industries, and for numerous reasons: The Baby Boomers are preparing for retirement, inheriting value as their parents leave them their homes (which will often be sold, with much of their value reinvested in mutual funds) and money. Many estimate a trillion-dollar inheritance, and I have no doubt that much of that, too, will find its way into mutual funds.

There is still more. Interest rates hit 45-year lows in late 1996, which pretty well destroyed any last resistance to purchasing mutual funds and to "borrowing to invest" (quite the opposite of what Michael and I encountered with the 20%+ interest rates in Canada back in the early 1980s).

And then there are what I call the GIC Refugees, who are marching into mutual fund salespeople's offices across North America as they find themselves with no alternative but to do what they should have been doing for the past 10, 20, even 30 years; they come out of desperation, and many see mutual funds as their salvation. And they are probably correct in that assumption.

The best kind of mutual funds give their investors a broad cross-section of financial services companies (such as Mackenzie stock, AGF stock, Trimark stock, Dundee Bancorp stock, etc.), along with other businesses that, in many ways, behave as the booming mutual funds industry does: revenue-generating, revenue-stream businesses such as cable and telecommunications.

So the wise mutual fund investor gets a diverse portfolio of businesses in the best of the mutuals available today.

But without mutual fund companies' stocks in one's

financial portfolio, one is truly missing the boat, as the often-brilliant Mr. Lynch admitted doing.

Oh, I should note one more thing. That boat is forever leaving the dock, yet it is always there for the boarding. Of course it is now "too late" to buy Trimark at its original $12, or even its present value of nearly $100 (when you figure in all the splits and dividends). But it will keep going up, not unlike Coke, Gillette, and other great businesses on the stock markets of the world. It's never, ever too late to buy into a quality company and own a share of greatness.

Can you think of any reason why these financial institutions won't keep increasing in price and value? I certainly cannot. Not with tens of millions of Baby Boomers waking up to their rapidly approaching retirements, governments cutting back on pensions and social programs, hundreds of billions of dollars in inheritances being left by parents for their children and grandchildren, and a world always thirsting for more soft drinks, more razor blades, more newspapers and magazines, more hamburgers, more insurance, more clothing — and, of course, more quality stocks and superior mutual funds.

13

Systematic
Withdrawal Plans

S INCE I have been stressing at great length, throughout
this book, how crucial it is for every investor to buy and
hold good, quality businesses (e.g., common stocks and/or
mutual funds that hold the common stocks of those superior
firms), I am often asked by my clients, "But how do I live?
Where will I get the money for vacations, for that automobile that needs replacing, for my child's wedding? I can't
simply sock away all of my savings into stocks and mutuals
forever, even though you keep insisting that one should hold
investments for that long."

The answer is not only simple but remarkably money-
saving — because it allows every one of us to legally keep
our taxes low while maintaining the vast majority of our capital in those investments as they continue growing and
thriving.

The answer (see the title of this chapter) is systematic

withdrawal plans, available from every broker and mutual fund dealer in Canada. Trimark, which runs some of the most successful and best-run mutual funds in the world, puts out a "taxation bulletin" that notes that "many Trimark unitholders have Systematic Withdrawal Plans that enable them to receive payments from their accounts on a monthly, quarterly or semi-annual basis." And so, they answer — in rather stiff and legal language — the questions most frequently asked about the tax treatment of these plans. Here is a taste of what they have to say:

> Each systematic withdrawal is considered a redemption of units from a unitholder's account. A capital gain or loss is calculated as the difference between the total proceeds received (i.e., the systematic payments) and the average cost of the units redeemed. The average cost per unit at the time of redemption is the total cost at which all units were purchased before the redemption, divided by the total number of units outstanding at the time. An estimate of the realized capital gain or loss is provided to unitholders on a semi-annual basis on their account statements.

Are you lost yet? This is why taxation people should not write books. But the point being made here is essential, in spite of its dryness. When a person has a systematic withdrawal plan — assuming, of course, that it is from a successful, decent portfolio, such as the mutual funds I will be referring to below — they need not fear that they are depleting the capital of their investment.

This is crucially important, because it may come as a

surprise to many readers. After all, if you pump water from a swimming pool, do you not eventually reach the bottom? If you take clothes from a closet, one by one, is it not eventually empty?

The answer in the case of excellent mutual funds and stocks is a resounding no, for the simple reason that while you are slowly and regularly withdrawing funds from your portfolio (as opposed to that swimming pool or closet), the money that remains in those financial vehicles is continuing to grow.

And grow.

And grow.

The following few examples may astonish you; I certainly hope that they bring you pleasure — as they have for many tens of thousands of wise investors.

How a Systematic Withdrawal Plan Worked with the Trimark Fund over a 15-Year Period

Trimark mutual funds began two funds that same day, September 1, 1981. Let us say that you invested $100,000 at the very inception of the Trimark [mutual] Fund, and have chosen to withdraw $825 every month, beginning 30 days after you invested $100,000; since the fund was "front end loaded," your account value dropped to $96,000 on the very first day, due to the 4% commission rate. Over the years, there would be capital gains distributions, changes (both up and down) in unit value, and more. Yet every reader of (and believer in) the principles expressed throughout this book would have ignored those daily fluctuations, would have ignored the "scoreboard" (the mutual fund listings in the daily newspapers), and let that $100,000 investment grow and compound over those 15 years — while withdrawing that regular, monthly amount of $825.

Here are a few highlights from that experience to savour. On December 31, 1983, after just over two years of withdrawing monthly, the value of your account was up to $155,387. On December 31, 1988, five years later, your fund value had reached $218,228. On December 31, 1993, five years after that — and after nearly a dozen years of withdrawing $9900 every single year — the Trimark Fund Account had a value of $410,854.

And on June 30, 1996, your original $100,000 — in spite of your withdrawing over $140,000 over all those years, had magically turned into $565,091.

It is essential to emphasize here that in both of these cases, if you had put your $100,000 into a comparable plan that paid a fixed 10% return, you would have been able to withdraw those monthly amounts, of course, but you would have been left with $90,349 in your savings. That's right: Your initial capital investment would have dropped nearly 10% over those same 15 years, instead of doubling, even quintupling.

What a difference!

How About if You Chose Templeton Two Decades Earlier?

If the above numbers and descriptions of a successful systematic withdrawal plan have not impressed you very much, let me truly blow you away with the following example of a very wise investor who was fortunate enough to have $100,000 to spare back in 1964 and chose to invest in the

Templeton Growth Fund, one of the greatest mutual funds of all time.

We will work this example almost the same way. You invest the sum, on January 2, 1964, and begin withdrawing, monthly, the sum of $750 a month (or $9000 annually) at once. In this case as well, all distributions of the fund will be reinvested, but we have chosen to index to inflation your withdrawals, so, for example, your $9000 of withdrawal in the first year will reach $14,662 annually by 1975, $34,959 by 1985, and over $50,000 by 1995, in order to allow you to live in the way to which you are accustomed. Okay? Now here goes (hold on tight): At the end of your first year in the Templeton Growth Fund, in which you withdrew that $9000, the cash value in your fund already hit $114,264, thanks to a rate of return of 28.40% that their brilliant managers achieved over those initial 12 months.

Let's talk about a "bad year" for a moment, since I do not wish to leave readers with the belief that even the most superior mutual funds go up only in a straight line. Managers are human; stock markets and stock prices go up and down; "corrections" are inevitable. In 1970, during which time you withdrew $10,965 (since your monthly withdrawal is indexed to the inflation rate, as noted above), the rate of return of the Templeton Growth Fund was minus 11.83%. Yet in spite of that, the cash value of your fund has now reached $141,665.

Jumping to 1980: You withdraw $22,834 over that difficult year of runaway inflation (during which the Canadian Consumer Price Index shot up a whopping 11.2%), yet the cash value of your Templeton Growth Fund account is now an impressive $768,362. (Oh, yes — its rate of return hit 28.6% that year.)

One could do this for every year, but let's leap to 1994, when you withdraw an indexed-to-inflation $49,340 over those 12 months. The rate of return of the Templeton Growth Fund was only 3.8%, which must have been disappointing. But you are not upset. You have withdrawn over $770,000 over the 31 years since you first invested that $100,000 in 1964, which has allowed you to buy the occasional gift for a friend, and maybe a trinket or two for your wife and children. And what is the cash value of your Templeton Growth Fund at the end of 1994?

Thanks to an average compound return of 17.09% over those three-plus decades, you now have a remaining cash value of $3,544,887. You read right: Over $3.5 million in net asset value.

If you are as dazzled by these numbers as most of my clients have been, then let me frighten you a bit as well. For the smart men and women at Templeton also chose to set up a parallel situation: someone who invested $100,000 that same day in 1964, but in an investment "opportunity" that paid exactly 10% — indexed to inflation, of course, to be fair in the comparison.

Here's the horror part. That person who "avoided all risks" by sinking his or her $100,000 back in 1964 into that "safe" and "reliable" and *guaranteed* 10% investment vehicle — while withdrawing the same amount per month as our friend who "risked" investing in the Templeton Growth Fund — hit a *peak* cash value in his account of $103,546 in 1968, but then the account began to diminish by larger and larger amounts. By 1973, the original $100,000 investment had dropped to $98,081. By 1979, the "capital" had dwindled to $47,141. And by 1981, the original investment (invested at

10%, indexed to inflation) had completely vanished, and the "cash value" was in negative territory: minus $1085.

That's right, good reader. The fear-of-risk investor out of money completely in less than a dozen years.

Want another scare? If that super-safe investor in the 10%-guaranteed vehicle continued to withdraw the same amounts as his friend invested in Templeton Growth Fund, by 1994 — when his daredevil buddy now had a "nest egg" of over $3.5 million — he had an "overdraft" of $518,476.

So much for the safety of guaranteed vehicles, such as GICs, savings bonds, and the like. So much for them — and so little from them. (See Chapter 14.)

Another major advantage of systematic withdrawal plans is that the money you regularly "take out" from your financial portfolio is taxed at a much lower rate than it would be as pure capital gains; it's considered the return on your principal — part of your original investment. So you would be taxed by your partner at Revenue Canada or the Internal Revenue Service far less harshly than if you, say, bought and sold a stock for a "quick killing" and withdrew your profit at one fell swoop — or earned interest income on a GIC or bond, which is taxed 100%.

Just as buying and holding quality businesses (or superior mutual funds that buy and hold quality businesses) is the wisest way to invest, so systematic withdrawal plans are the wisest way to redeem your ever-growing portfolio. Go over the examples I gave you from Trimark and Templeton mutual funds, above, and never forget this key thought: When you are redeeming a set amount every month of your mutual funds units, the remaining units over time will increase in value much faster than you can redeem them. In all my years of assisting my clients, we have never once exhausted a client's principal, because the pool never runs dry and the closet is never empty.

But What If That Dreaded Market Correction Occurs?

Once again, fear raises its ugly head, and we all know what President Roosevelt said about it, back in the dark days before the Second World War, that fear is the only thing we should ever fear.

So the market suffers a severe "correction." (As it's done dozens of times over this century, as I pointed out in an earlier chapter.) So countless stocks and mutual funds take a severe hit, and drop (seemingly) precipitously. This does not mean that one should alter the systematic withdrawal plan, any more than it means that one should call one's broker and scream, "Sell!"

Ignore the stock market downturn. Ignore the Antichrists and naysayers of the newspapers and magazines. Continue your systematic withdrawal plan and stop checking "the scoreboard," because the value of your mutual funds and the value of your stocks and the value of your financial portfolio will turn around and come back — they always have and they always will.

The truth of the above depends on several salient points, however: That you have not been diversifying wildly (by spreading your money over a half dozen funds or more, as so many financial planners foolishly suggest. That you have been avoiding the latest "hot" mutual fund or get-rich-quick penny stock tips. And that you have been investing — long-term investing — in quality mutual funds such as the ones whose remarkable records I have noted in this chapter, for instance, Trimark or Templeton. Or AIC funds or the new Infinity family, for example, all of which put their money into superior businesses with decades-long brilliant track records, such as Coca-Cola, Gillette, and, yes, Berkshire Hathaway, Warren Buffett's holding company.

A portfolio consisting of rock-solid businesses and mutual funds can never become worthless (which is every investor's worst nightmare); it simply cannot happen. Your systematic withdrawal plan should continue to redeem money for you regularly, and your high-quality financial portfolio will continue to grow as the stock markets of the world will inevitably march onward and upward — as they always have.

Still not "sold" on buying (quality) common stocks and mutual funds rather than "risk-free" investments such as Guaranteed Income Certificates and United States and Canada Savings Bonds? Read the next chapter and smile. (Or weep, if you've traditionally gone the "guaranteed" way.)

14

Concentrate,
Don't Diversify

R EMEMBER the famous quotation, "There are three kinds of lies: lies, damned lies, and statistics." But statistics actually often tell profound truths, as do charts. And charts of the way stock markets move, and the way successful stocks move, can be very informative indeed.

The headline on the front page of the November 29, 1996, *Globe and Mail* Report on Business section read "TSE Shatters 6000" with a chart right below it, covering the years 1970 to the present. I needn't reproduce it for you to be able to declare that it's no straight line but rather a lot of jagged edges.

So while the Toronto Stock Exchange "composite index" of 300 stocks was at 1012 in 1977, just 36 months later it broke 2000. Another 74 months later, in March 1986, it broke 3000; 16 months later (in July 1987), it moved past 4000. It took another 102 months, until February 1996, to make it to

5000, and then only 10 months more to reach the latest "magical" number of 6000. And, of course, the TSE spent most of 1999 above the once-impossible 7000 mark.

Over that same period of a quarter century plus, there were several recessions (in 1970, 1974, 1979, 1981-82, and 1989-91), as well as a rather diverse collection of prime ministers who "ran" this country, building up deficits and playing with interest rates through the Bank of Canada: Pierre Trudeau, Joe Clark, Trudeau again, John Turner, quickly followed by Brian Mulroney, Kim Campbell, rapidly replaced by Jean Chrétien. The United States saw the presidencies of Nixon, Ford, Carter, Reagan, Bush, and Clinton.

Yet throughout all the recessions, all the procession of political leaders, the composite index of 300 stocks on the TSE zigged and zagged its way up that huge, steep mountain. The zigs are applauded by everyone, of course, but the zags often scare the hell out of investors — and you've seen in this book how low my opinion of fear is, when it comes to intelligent investing. Fear is its enemy and destroyer.

Here's my favourite "milestone" in that inexorable climb of the TSE to its record height of 6000 in late November 1996, as recorded by journalists Angela Barnes and Diana Clifford in the *Globe and Mail*: "July 15, 1996: The composite gets caught up in the sell-off in the United States and loses 86 points, dropping to 4,955. The Dow Jones Industrial average in New York slumps 161 points to 5,350 in what market analysts are sure is the start of the long-awaited correction. History proves otherwise."

The market analysts were "sure" — and I'm sure that thousands of brokers phoned tens of thousands of their clients that afternoon, to beg them to sell — while happily gobbling up their commissions on each sale. But they were wrong. And they were fearful. And that single day — July 15, 1996 — was arguably the best day to purchase quality stocks and mutual funds at a good or at least lower price, that entire, record-setting year.

I have always felt that the vast majority of people set up their investments lacking the correct, positive attitude of "investing to become wealthy." They do quite the opposite, in fact: They set up their financial portfolios out of fear of losing their money.

So what do they do? They buy bonds. They buy GICs. They buy Canada and U.S. Savings Bonds. They buy all of these "guaranteed" investment vehicles that, in fact, have very little true growth potential. Alas, the stockbroker or investment advisor who is setting up that portfolio with that nervous, negative client doesn't want to lose her, much less get sued. So he invariably creates a portfolio with a huge diversification, and very little concentration.

Most portfolios are far too diversified. Isn't it interesting that wealthy people rarely have much, if any, diversification in their financial ownership? Indeed, the majority of the Super Rich have their money sunk into one business. Think of Frank Stronach, who does not put his money in dozens of different companies; he owns a company called Magna, since he buys and holds his own firm, has faith in it, and puts his money where his mouth and his time and his soul are.

The same can be said of Ken Thomson (with his Canadian newspapers, his legal publishing firm, The Bay department stores) and Bill Gates (Microsoft), and, of course, Warren Buffett (Berkshire Hathaway). As Buffett writes in his annual report, "We eat our own cooking." And wouldn't you rather feast in a fine restaurant where the chef cannot wait to sit down to a meal he has prepared himself than in an eatery where the cook sends out for a pizza?

It is not only individual investors like you and me who tend to over-diversify; so do far too many "managers" of mutual funds. No point in being a hero and risking every-thing, they seem to be saying. Let's buy stocks — lots and lots of stocks — and hope that at least a few turn out to be winners. Indeed, the traditional mutual fund holds three, four, even five dozen stocks and more, always diversifying to cover their assets (vulgar pun intended).

GICs and CSBs Are *Not* Good Investments

During the same week that the TSE composite shot past 6000, I heard some pretty amazing declarations on Canadian radio, and then read similar thoughts in some daily newspa-pers, which forced me to accept that my ears weren't lying to me.

Here is essentially what some experts declared, in my own paraphrase: "You know, you're actually doing better today with your GIC, which millions purchase in order to obtain 'regular' income. Back in the early 1980s, when Canada Savings Bonds paid 19% and GICs were around 15%, inflation was around 12%, so your after-tax return was infinitesimal; you really weren't making any money at all. But today, you lucky kid, you, inflation is only 1% and we're paying you around 3% on your GIC, so after taxes you're making nearly 1% a year. You're doing so much better."

Can you believe this? It reminds me of what a nutritionist once wrote about white bread that brags that it's "fortified with over 30 vitamins." Sure, the health food advocate declared, those bakers are showing sensitivity to your health by putting all those vitamins into their bread. What they never tell you is that they refine all the nutrients out of the flour before they bake it so that it loses nearly all of its value; only then do they put in the vitamins. Should we thank the bakers for putting back in the vitamins they had removed?

The banks apparently think that we should thank them. Let's think back to those magnificent Canada Savings Bonds the banks eagerly flogged to their unsuspecting customers in the early 1980s. Ottawa actually offered 19.5% in interest on CSBs that year, and the citizens of this great land were so impressed with this astonishingly high rate that the government had to actually put a limit on how much each person could buy. (I think it was around $15,000, but who cares?)

Was this as good a deal as it sounded at the time? Quite the opposite. If you adjust that rate for taxes and inflation — let's say you are in the 50% tax bracket — that glorious 19.5% interest now drops by half, to only 9.75%. And since inflation that terrible year was a towering 12.5%, all that those wonderful CSBs with the great rates accomplished for you was a loss of over 3% that year.

A loss of 3%! On $100,000 invested in Canada Savings Bonds that year — assuming that you were "lucky" enough to buy that high an amount — you lost $3000. Gee, you could have probably done better with the slot machines down in Vegas. So much for those thrilling interest rates of yesteryear. So much for the way most people felt, that it was "wonderful to buy a savings bond" that year.

No, it's not fraud. But it sure is stupidity. It was simply an ugly case of the government of Canada needing the public to finance the bad management of their monetary affairs. A government touting savings bonds is really no different than a person overspending each month and then going to his bank and exclaiming, "I overspent and I really need to borrow some money to make my mortgage payment." It was simply bad behaviour on the government's part, since if it ever learned to live within its means, it would not need to borrow from the public. This is precisely what savings bonds are all about: big governments — whether Ottawa, Washington, or London — borrowing money from Peter to pay for Paul's dreadful spending habits. Brilliant. Simply brilliant.

And the government of Canada has not really acted with any more honesty since then — and the banks have continued to flog their dreadful, dog-food product. So, if you purchased Canada Savings Bonds (series 42) in 1987, you earned 9% that year, 10.16% the following year, and a whopping 10.91% the following year, followed by 10.75% the next. But how about the years after that? Well, in 1991, your interest rate on S42 bonds dropped to 7.5%, then to 6% in 1992, and only 5.125% in 1993. Figure in the income tax on that, and the inflation rates of those same years (the latter drifted between 4% and 5.6% through 1991, before it finally fell below 2% in 1992), and you can see how lousily you did. If you made any money at all.

I could do the same with year after year of CSBs, but let me just jump to November 1996 and their series S51: That series of bonds promised 3% for the last two months of that year, then a "leap" to 4% for 1997, 5% in 1998, 6% in 1999, and a giant 6.5% in the year 2000. Once again, if you figure in taxes and even a presumably low interest rate, you are making only pennies on this so-called trustworthy savings vehicle. And Series 58, announced in February 1999, had a 10-year term to maturity and carried an interest rate of 3.65% for the first year. Big deal.

"Risky" Bank Stocks or "Guaranteed" Investments?

Many years ago, there used to be a common warning to young women who chose to "move in" with their boyfriends without the latter making a commitment to marriage. It was a bit crude, but had a lot of truth to it: "Why should he buy the cow when the milk is free?" Why should this guy ever marry you? He's getting what he wants without the promise, the engagement ring, the wedding.

I thought of that old expression (which is probably still used, along with a wagging finger, by many a parent to their daughters today) because it echoed in my mind when I thought of the absurdity of anyone's purchasing Guaranteed Income Certificates over the stock of the bank that issues these horrible financial vehicles: "Why buy the milk from a bad investment when you can get the cow that offers it?"

The milk is those lousy GICs that so many Canadians have counted on for "guaranteed," "regular," and "risk-free" income, and the magnificent, handsome pedigree cows (banks) that are forever increasing in value, making huge profits, 14% interest. Of course, the inflation rate was nearly 11% that year in Canada, but they never remind you of that; so with taxes and inflation, you actually lost money over those 12 months.

That same year, you could have taken the same money that you could have put into that TD GIC and purchased that bank's common shares on the Toronto Stock Exchange instead. The price: $6.63 per share. The price of each share, exactly 12 months later? Way up to $8.25 — an increase of over 20% — and that doesn't include the dividends the bank paid that year on each share of its common stock.

I should mention that the price of a single share of Toronto Dominion Bank on the TSE broke $20 in 1993, reached $24 by 1995, and as of the fall of 1999 was over $30. Of course, you could always have bought a GIC from TD in 1996, while its stock price was shooting up over 50%, and have gotten a rate of 3%, if so desired. But why desire that rotten deal at all?

Let's have some similar fun with the Bank of Montreal. In 1984, you could have purchased some GICs from that fine bank and received a generous 10.5%; not bad, you think. Of course, the shares of that bank — so risky, being the stock market, as we all know so well — were going for $12.75 a share. (Oh, yes — inflation that year was down to below 5%; lucky you.) One year later, you may choose to cash in your safe, guaranteed GIC and get that wonderful 10%+ interest, losing only half to inflation, and another half, if not more, to income tax. Or you could check your stock market prices and discover that those shares of Bank of Montreal going for $12.75 in 1984 were now up to $17.25 — over 33% higher than a year earlier. Were you crazy?

Let's do one more bank; if this doesn't win you over, what will? Let's choose the year 1989 this time. You take out a GIC from the Royal Bank, Canada's largest and often most successful financial institution, and you get nearly 11% interest on it. Fabulous — if you ignore the 5% inflation rate that year.

Of course, you could have bought shares in the same

bank offering you that GIC on the Toronto Stock Exchange; they would have cost you $25 each. Today, in late 1999, you can always renew that great GIC and receive nearly 5% interest on it. Of course, the shares of Royal Bank stock have done slightly better — they broke $50 in late November 1996 and $60 in March 1997, up rather pleasingly from $31.13 a share at the end of 1995. And in late 1999, their stock was over $60 a share.

And please don't forget that every one of the major banks of Canada not only has seen its common shares zooming upward over the past several years, but is regularly offering dividends on each share as well — leaving the miserable rates on each bank's GICs in the dust and far behind. Zooming upward? More like blasting off. Here are some more numbers to savour. In 1979, you could have bought shares of Bank of Nova Scotia from a broker for $8.13 a share; in late 1996, the price of each share pushed past $46. In early 1998, its stock split two-for-one, and at the end of the century it was hovering around $33 a share. In those same two years, you could have bought common shares in the Bank of Commerce for $12.81 and $61.10, respectively. In early 1997, its shares split two-for-one, and it is now is around $30 a share.

What have I been showing you? That everyone — from teenagers to Generation Xers to Baby Boomers to retirees — should never buy term deposits or T-bills or Canada Savings Bonds or GICs offered by their local bank; they should be investing *in* banks. Buy bank stocks — not their crummy products. That's where the money is; buy the cow itself, not the sour milk they are forever pushing you to purchase.

Here's my point, captured in a single, stunning example.

On November 25, 1996, you could have purchased a GIC from any of Canada's top five banks and got something like 3% interest — probably a bit less. Yet on that same day, November 25, 1996, every one of those giant banks saw their common stock go up an average of 3%. The Bank of Montreal's stock jumped $1.80 per share, to $44.65; the Royal's shares went up $2.10, to $48.75; Toronto Dominion leapt $1.70, to $36.20; the Bank of Nova Scotia moved up $1.50, to hit $46.05; the Canadian Imperial Bank of Commerce shot ahead $1.85, to $59.10.

There you have it: 3% a year on their GICs, or 3% in a single day, with every one of their common stocks.

Is there really a choice here?

Two Very Telling Letters from the Not-So-Distant Past

I recently came across two quite extraordinary letters that were exchanged between a typical Canadian citizen and a typical Canadian bank. And this was not so long ago, the fall of 1983. I shall leave the names off "to protect the innocent," but I believe that this dialogue captures both pithily and painfully what I have been saying over the last few pages.

September 16, 1983

Bank of Montreal
Shareholders Services Division
First Canadian Place
Toronto, Ontario

Dear Mr. _____,

In 1952 my father retired from farming and had a house and roughly $100,000. He invested in Canada Savings Bonds and similar investments. Mother is still living and she has made similar investments.

Now instead of this type of investment, had Father bought $100,000 worth of Bank of Montreal shares, we would obviously be better off to-day. Can you tell me how many shares we would have today? If you can give me the dividend history over that period it would be appreciated. I personally have 1600 common shares of Bank of Montreal and 500 of your preferred stock.

Your help regarding the above would be most appreciated.

And here is the reply to that letter:

October 24, 1983

Dear Mr. _____,

I must apologize for the delay in responding to your recent question concerning your father's investments. As you have no doubt noticed, we have been involved in a strategic expansion into the United States . . .

In 1952, your father could have acquired roughly 3400 shares which, after a five-for-one split in 1967, would be 17,000 shares today, with a current market value of $456,875 (at the $26.875 close of business price, October 20, 1983). In computing this value, we have not taken into consideration a further $410,093 of dividends that would have been earned since that time. Unfortunately, we do not have any way of reflecting your father's individual tax position so we cannot determine how many shares he might have bought out of his net dividends.

I hope this is helpful to you.

How's that for an interesting statement about the advantages of purchasing the common shares of banks, rather than their highly dubious products?

Sometimes I think of banks in the same way that I think of tobacco companies. They hook you when young, and you become emotionally, if not physically, addicted to them. In the case of the latter, you know what I'm talking about. Smoking is "cool." The guy with the cigarette gets the girl, or at the very least, lassoes the horse. And Joe Camel is such a cute cartoon character, isn't he?

Look at what banks do. They flood the grade schools with colouring books; they fill every parent's mind with the belief that "if you don't teach your kids to put their birthday money into a savings account (paying ½%, maybe 1%, if you're really fortunate), then you are an abusive mummy or daddy."

So we all get "hooked" on banks and banking and banking products. And then they "have" us for life, to purchase blindly their products and services while making their shareholders, instead of us, wealthy.

No, banks don't cause cancer or heart disease or emphysema. But if the public continues to buy their line about "you're far safer with a CSB/GIC," then they are only asking to end up as "refugees," hammering on the doors of their financial planners, begging them to help them out. Their GICs, which paid them 5.5% back in 1994, just came due, and they can't get much over 4% on the renewal. Their earnings have just dropped nearly one-third, and they can't make ends meet. What should they do?

What should they do? Read this chapter — and buy bank stocks. They are the real cash cows.

Are RRSPs the Best Way to Go?

Every January and February, Canadians probably see the letters "RRSP" more frequently than the words "McDonald's"
or "Donuts." (In the U.S., it's "IRAs".) And we all know why.
In those two months, tens of billions of dollars are poured
into Registered Retirement Savings Plans, out of the fervent
— if not necessarily realistic — hope that a few thousand
dollars tucked away each winter (tax-free!) will eventually
amount to enough for them and their spouses to live on after
retirement.

Now, there is nothing wrong with RRSPs, except I'd like
to make a brief argument here that there isn't much right
with them, either. Indeed, a very, very strong argument can
be made for leveraging — in other words, borrowing — to
invest on your own, rather than socking away a few grand
annually into an RRSP.

In order to do this clearly, allow me to set up two straw
men. Person A puts a $12,000 contribution into his RRSP,
and person B borrows $150,000 from a bank at 5% (or 8%,
or whatever the rate is at the time). Let's first discuss
what these two men and their two investment plans have in
common.

Person A's $12,000 RRSP contribution is a kind of forced
savings; so is Person B's borrowing the $150,000 from his
bank, at least in this case.

Person A's $12,000 has a tax deferral, of course; that's
much of the charm and value of RRSPs. But Person B actually can write off that $150,000 loan as a tax deduction, not
unlike the way that Americans may deduct their mortgage
payments on their houses.

Finally, both Person A and Person B have one thing perfectly in common: Each of their investments will now undergo tax-free compounding.

Okay, so what are the pitfalls of Person A's RRSP contribution, and what are the benefits of Person B's $150,000 bank loan? You may find some of them surprising:

Here's the first one. Person A must put a minimum of 80% of his RRSP contribution each year into Canadian stocks and bonds — that's four-fifths! — into a country that handles only 2% of the world's trading in commodities. (There's nothing wrong with investing in one's country — but 80 cents of every dollar?)

Not so with Person B, who is free to invest all 100% of his loan anywhere in this very exciting globe: China, Japan, England, South Africa, Israel, South America — anywhere.

There's another important difference between our two men. The RRSP of Person A has absolutely zero collateral value. If he wishes to borrow to invest in a business or for any reason, whether he has $10 or $10 million in his RRSP, it has absolutely no value as collateral. And Person B? His $150,000 has full collateral value, which could prove crucial at any point in his lengthy business or family life.

Here's one that may really throw you: When Person A eventually begins to withdraw his RRSP, every penny will be 100% taxable. Not so with Person B, who took out the loan. The return of his principal is tax-free, and when he makes a profit — which he undoubtedly will, if he follows the suggestions made in this book — his capital gains are only 75% taxable. So, if he withdraws, say, $20,000 in capital gains, he will pay taxes on only $15,000; quite an advantage over his RRSP-loving friend, Person A.

Other pitfalls for the more-travelled route of Person A and his RRSP are more obvious. RRSPs are government-controlled, of course. No government controls anything Person B does with his money.

And there are maximum contribution limits for any RRSP, which are always changing, but still always limited to a small percentage of a person's annual earnings. Not so with Person B, who has no maximum limits whatsoever on the amount he chooses to borrow from the bank and invest anywhere in the world.

Another pitfall for Person A is that, should he choose at any time to borrow to invest in his RRSP, the interest on that loan is not tax-deductible. Yet it is quite the opposite for Person B, whose interest on his loan is fully tax-deductible — as are all investment loans.

Furthermore, RRSPs assume that Canadians will be in a lower tax bracket when they retire — something that is hardly true for most of us, especially those who have invested well. But Person B's plan allows him, and all Canadians who choose to go his way, to plan for a retirement lifestyle that they can look forward to.

Finally, Person A's RRSP route — surely the road most frequently travelled by Canadians — has but a small capital amount working for him, which is a definite pitfall. But Person B, with his tax-deductible bank loan of $150,000, has a large capital amount working for him, and one that can do brilliantly, when not limited to Canadian purchases. His capital has full collateral value; is only 75% taxable on its capital gains; is not government controlled; has no contribution limits. And the interest on his loan is tax deductible.

The winner? As they announce at boxing matches, I

suggest that it is clearly Person B (and by a knock-out) with his bank loan, over Person A, with his small, annual contributions to his RRSP. Remember, I'm not saying that RRSPs are worthless or harmful. I am suggesting that leveraging oneself (see the chapters above on the Laws of Wealth Creation) is always the way to go, in order to guarantee a comfortable, even lavish, retirement — and not the much-touted RRSP. I want to challenge the conventional wisdom here, and put it as clearly as I can: RRSP contributions are simply not sufficient for your future happiness and financial security.

15

On Diversification

A S an investment advisor, I see investors who have been promised security and safety through excessive diversification. There is a false sense of security that has been created through the panacea of "diversifying one's risk" through the purchase of a package of mutual funds (most of which, of course, will already be diversified in themselves).

The purpose of this chapter is to discuss just how much or how little diversification can be a preservative against risk when stock markets are venturing into uncertain territory. Also, I would like to discuss whether or not increased diversification (through holding too many mutual funds) is simply creating a closet index situation. By this, I mean that you are paying management fees to mimic a stock market index, while at the same time distorting potentially good returns that you could have obtained with far less diversification.

Don't get me wrong. Some diversification is wise. Otherwise

you risk your capital with only one or two stocks. The question is: How much is prudent?

Charles Ellis, a partner of Greenwich Associates in Connecticut, is a leading authority in investment research. In a recent article from the *Financial Analysts' Journal*, he states that he is not convinced that the simple answer to the inherent difficulty of investing is to diversify. He recalls the famous American journalist, H.L. Mencken, who admonished, "For every complicated problem, there is a simple answer. And it's wrong."

For starters, Ellis argues that a long list of holdings is no more "portfolio diversification" than the beautiful Chartres Cathedral in France is a huge pile of stones. Both need deliberate design and skilful construction. Ellis's next word of warning is to his fellow professionals: "Increasing the number of holdings dilutes knowledge, disperses research efforts, distracts attention, and diminishes determination to act — when called for — decisively and with dispatch."

Warren Buffett believes that diversification is a protection against one's own ignorance, and the need to diversify goes down significantly if you don't feel you're ignorant! Ellis argues that the more investors diversify, the more they increase the risk of not knowing as much about each investment, thus getting left behind when others who know more act on their better knowledge.

What is more important than the number of holdings is that they be different. Ellis believes protection against one's own sins of commission usually needs fewer than a dozen different security positions. Increase that number, and you increase your uncertainty more rapidly than you decrease risk. And as the implicit cost of diversification soars (in that the proportional gain from your winners decreases), so the benefit of risk reduction decelerates inversely.

The more you spread yourself, Ellis argues, the less ready you will be to take pre-emptive action when a particular holding turns sour and the more you must rely on other people's research.

He cites two excellent examples of professional investors who have made a virtue of limiting their holdings to what they know. One is Philip Fisher, who has had a huge influence in shaping Warren Buffett's investment philosophy. He has written much about, and also put into practice, the merits of owning the stocks of just a few truly outstanding companies and concentrating on becoming expert enough in each of them to stay serenely committed for the long haul.

The other, as you may have guessed, is Warren Buffett himself. The outstanding performance of his investment company, Berkshire Hathaway, is only too evident. He has had phenomenal success, as I've noted throughout this book, as suggested by one of my favourite statistics: The cost of one share of Berkshire Hathaway in 1965 was $12; in April 1999, that single share was worth over $72,000.

Buffett likes to advise investors to visualize themselves as having a lifetime "decision ticket" with only 20 numbers to punch. Each time you make a decision, you punch your ticket, and after the 20th punch you must leave the game. Buffett believes that an investor would take far more care in making any investment decision if he realized that he had a limited number of decisions when investing. Ellis notes that Buffett has gone as far as declaring four of Berkshire Hathaway's investments to be permanent — Coca-Cola Co., Walt Disney Co., GEICO Corp., and the Washington Post Co.

As Ellis asks, how many scientists make more than a dozen important discoveries in their careers? Or how many authors write a dozen great books?

And how many investors understand the importance of making their best investments the biggest? It is a thought worth pondering, when it comes from an expert's expert, who has seen the creed of diversification both wax and wane in his lifetime.

In a recent annual report from Berkshire Hathaway, Buffett sneered at the issue of portfolio rebalancing. Many times, an excellent holding will rise to dominate one's portfolio. An "investor" will choose to sell off shares of this excellent holding, instead of loading up on this stock, simply to "bring their portfolio back into balance." This, of course, makes no sense to Warren Buffett. He compares this behaviour to the great coach of the championship basketball team the Chicago Bulls pulling Michael Jordan from the game because he is scoring too many points and has become too valuable to the team.

I believe that investors are holding many different mutual funds because they are not confident about owning one really good one. They diversify, but fail to realize that each mutual fund is diversified in itself.

Investors are providing themselves with a false sense of security, and are doing themselves far more harm than good. I have seen as many as 20 different mutual funds in a $40,000 portfolio. And I have seen as many as 40 different mutual funds in a $1-million portfolio.

The catch is, the typical mutual fund will hold as many as 100 different stocks — indeed, some hold even more. So, the investor who owns 10 to 20 different mutual funds ends up holding (literally!) thousands of stocks, without realizing it. This investor is hardly protecting himself against losses by doing this. He is simply "di-worse-ifying" because invariably he has too much money in his mediocre investments, and not enough in the really good ones. I believe that a portfolio of mutual funds of between three and five will give you more than enough diversification, and at the same time will give you the concentration that will produce superior returns over time. This will be especially true if the mutual funds chosen are practising a management style similar to that of the inspired Warren Buffett (buy-and-hold), rather than continually trading.

Modern proponents of this business perspective of investing Buffett-style include three very successful mutual funds. Robert Torray manages the Torray Fund in the United States. He has achieved a three-year annualized total return of 38.9%, as quoted in the *New York Times*. Part of the "trick," according to Mr. Torray, is the fund's concentrated portfolio: 20 stocks represent more than 70% of the fund's assets. He also thinks long term. After he finds a good company, he is willing to hold on to it, virtually indefinitely.

The AIC group of mutual funds has also borrowed its investment philosophy from Warren Buffett. The AIC Advantage Fund was the number one Canadian Equity Fund in Canada for a long time, averaging 22.7% for 10 years. It also ranked number one over a two-year period, achieving a return of 54.4% — not to mention 53.7% for three years and 36.3% for five years. (This was noted in the Financial Times Bell Charts, Canadian Equity Funds, March 31, 1998.) And while all of its funds' prices were hit hard during 1999, one has little doubt that it will return to greatness in the new century.

Another mutual fund company that bears mentioning is Infinity Mutual Funds (now Dynamic Infinity funds). Also modelling their investment philosophy after that of Warren Buffett, their rate of return year-to-date for the Infinity Canadian Fund was 48.8%; for Infinity Wealth Management, 43.1%; and for the International Fund, 47.1%. (This was as of April 22, 1998.) Infinity was also hurt by the lunacy of the stock market (and its absurd valuation of banking and wealth management stocks) in 1999, but it is on the road to recovery as I write.

Infinity was rated the second-best new mutual fund in Canada, according to the *Globe and Mail*. One should note that there are over 250 Canadian equity funds in Canada, and only 25 of them beat the TSE 300. Infinity Canadian came in at number four! Anyone care to predict how it will do early in the new millennium as financial stocks, mutual fund companies, and great blue chips such as Coke and Gillette start bouncing back, as they always have, and always will?

All of the above-mentioned mutual funds employ a buy-and-hold approach. As well, they have concentrated portfolios, with over 50% of their assets concentrated in their top 10 holdings. Clearly, Charles Ellis's theories work.

As I've noted, Infinity Mutual Funds, and AIC, and a number of other quality buy-and-hold investment vehicles (and many hundreds of high-quality stocks across North America) had rather distressing results in 1999 — but I don't believe that undercuts my arguments in this chapter at all. Why? Read the next chapter and you'll understand.

16

It's the Business, Not the Stock!

IT is time to learn how to discern the difference between fluctuation in stock prices and permanent principal losses: a morality tale of who has tenacity, who doesn't — and who gains the most.

Here is a powerful story for you. I may be simplifying it a bit, and rounding off numbers now and then, but I'm sure you'll find it informative and inspiring. You might wish to consider it a mystery, called "Whatever Happened to All the 1973 Investors?"

In 1973, a hundred citizens from all walks of life, from all across North America, heard about the legendary investor Warren Buffett. These men and women flew to Omaha, Nebraska, to attend one of his annual meetings, and were all enthralled by his presentation. And every one of them decided to invest in Berkshire Hathaway.

They all returned home. Some took out mortgages on

their homes, while others simply pulled money out of hefty bank accounts that hardly affected the balances. But they all had one thing in common: Every single one of them invested $100,000 in 1973, buying Berkshire at $80 a share.

Today — in the closing weeks of 1999 as I write these words — each one of those $80 shares is worth around $60,000. Or, to put it another way, those initial investments of $100,000, just over a quarter century ago, are now worth over $70 million.

Human nature being what it is, it's possible that there may be only *one* investor left of those original 100 in 1973 who held on to his or her initial investment and rode each of those $80 shares to a nearly 1000% increase.

Why only one of that original number? There are many reasons, and each of them underlines the central thesis of this book, that if you wish to become wealthy in the stock market, if you wish to invest the billionaire's way, then you must buy and hold, and invest from a business perspective.

And hold.

And hold.

Why did 99% of the original investors throw away the chance to earn those tens of millions?

One reason is that the price of the stock fell soon after its $80 debut. By 1974, it was down to $40 a share. You hardly need to be a philosopher or a rocket scientist to imagine what went through the minds of nearly every one of those original 100 investors: "My $100,000 is worth only $50,000 now!"

How many of those original investors "headed for the hills," to quote the old TV and movie westerns, as the stomach-churning fear of principal losses gripped them?

I would guess probably one-half of them — 50 — dumped their Berkshire Hathaway shares in 1974, less than a year after they made their initial $100,000 investment. And I can guess their reasoning: "Let's get out while the getting is good! Let's sell these shares before their value drops to zero! At least we can still recover $50,000 of our original investment."

As it happens, the shares of Berkshire Hathaway soon made a recovery, and once again reached the original price of $80.

How many of those initial investors (now down from 100 to 50) must have wiped their collective brows, looked at their spouses and their stockbrokers, and cried, "What a nasty experience that was. I'll *never* do that again. I got my money back. Let's get the hell out of Dodge City and put this dreadful thing behind us!"

For the sake of our example, let's say that another 50% bailed out at this stage, which puts our original 100 investors down to around 25.

Now, another common type of investor fear/investor greed took over when the Berkshire Hathaway stock hit $160 a share. The "value" of each share had doubled. And a different set of emotions kicked in. "How high can it possibly go?" most of the remaining investors thought to themselves. "I paid $80, it's dropped to $40, and now it's doubled from its original price, to $160. It could easily drop to $40 again. No, I'd better get out right now. After all, I can't go broke taking a profit!"

I would estimate that approximately another half of the original 100 investors — now down to 25 — headed for the door, selling their Berkshire Hathaway shares for twice their original investment.

This left around a dozen men and women who still held on to their shares of Buffett's dynamic young company.

The stock hit some $300 within the next few years. And you can just imagine the thoughts in the minds of most of the few remaining original purchasers of Berkshire Hathaway shares. "Whoever heard of a $300 stock? It's unbelievable. We've had a great ride, and we certainly can't go broke taking a profit!"

I'd like to suggest that we were, at this point, down to six people still holding their shares in Berkshire Hathaway out of the original 100.

When it hit $800 a share — 10 times the original investment — "a ten-bagger," as the great investor Peter Lynch likes to say — probably another three sold their original shares of Berkshire Hathaway.

Which brings us down to three people out of the initial 100 investors.

Let's not forget, stockbrokers have to make their commissions, don't they? They sold their clients these Berkshire Hathaway shares for $80 only a few years earlier and admirably urged them to hold on to the stock, through that frightening drop to $40, and to continue to hold, during that take-the-money-and-run rise to $300 a share. The broker made only a few grand of commission when the client first made that $100,000 purchase. But now, at $800 a share, how can even the finest, most stalwart broker not resist the urge to tell her client to sell? Of course, now that the shares are worth around a million dollars, the broker might make $25,000 in the sale of the Berkshire Hathaway shares, and another $25,000 in the redeployment of the money.

By the time Berkshire Hathaway hit $1000, certainly an

impressive figure for any stock on the New York exchange, I have little doubt that two of the last three remaining initial investors had sold all their shares, simply ecstatic that they made over a dozen times their original investment in just a few years.

And why not? Who ever heard of a stock that sells for $1000 a share?

Thus ends my little fable — which has a lot of truth in it. Only one investor stuck it out from 1974 to 1999 — a quarter century! — and held on to the original $100,000 worth of Berkshire Hathaway shares, purchased at what must have been seen back then as a very costly $80 a share. And that one single investor now owns over $70,000,000 in Berkshire Hathaway — including large chunks of Coca-Cola, Gillette, American Express, Dairy Queen, the seventh-largest automobile insurer in the United States (GEICO), and the second-largest reinsurers in the world (General Re), and dozens of other major companies that were not part of Berkshire Hathaway's holdings when the original investment was made.

And get this: When that single, very wise, very patient, very wealthy original investor picked up the daily newspaper in late October 1999, he saw that his beloved Berkshire Hathaway company had just shelled out $2.2 *billion* (you read right; $2.2 billion, plus the assumption of debt, making a total enterprise value of around $9 billion) to purchase a company called MidAmerican Energy Holdings Company. And he's excited that Mr. Buffett continues to deploy capital, and he's so happy that one more major firm is now under the giant umbrella of the business he stuck with, through thick and thin — mainly thick — since the mid-'70s.

When is the last time that *any* of the companies in which you own shares, took $2.2 *million*, much less $2.2 *billion*, or $9 billion, and added such quality and quantity to the value of your shares? What a powerful argument for not paying out dividends to shareholders (which are usually gobbled up in taxes, anyway), but rather using all profits to purchase more companies to add to its glorious holdings.

The Moral of This Strange Tale Should Be Clear by Now

As the great poet T.S. Eliot once wrote, this "leads us to an overwhelming question." And here it is: What was it that those 99 investors of the original 100 investors in Berkshire Hathaway in 1973 focused on, that drove each of them out — that scared them out — of their initial investment over that quarter century?

And, relatedly: What was it that the one investor who stuck through it all focused on, that kept him invested?

The answer to the first question is *the stock price*!

Ninety-nine people focused on the (absurd, unrelated-to-reality) stock price, and for that reason they either sold at a loss or sold at a modest profit. The price was "too low" or "too high" or "might drop to zero," or they accepted the old expression that "you can't go broke taking a profit," or . . . And even if they sold at a huge profit, it certainly wasn't anywhere near what the one, single, very wise investor made by sticking with Berkshire Hathaway for a quarter century.

That one, multi-multi-millionaire who stayed with Berkshire from 1974 to the end of the century did something different: *He focused on the business*. And there lies the true secret of successful investing: Investing the Billionaire's Way. (And don't forget the subtitle of this book, either: *The Genius of Patience.*)

It's the difference between true investing and merely speculating. It's the difference between discussing short-term performance and the economic fundamentals of the business we own. (Note that I wrote "the business we own," not "the stock I buy and sell, and which is worth such and such today, and was worth such and such yesterday, and I fear what it may be worth tomorrow.")

This brings me to my next point, on how the stock market works.

Do remember, the *business* kept only one person from those initial 100 investors "in"; the *stock market* scared away the 99 others. When we recall that, we truly understand how important it is to do what I've urged you to do, earlier in this book: *to turn off the stock market, and focus on the business behind the stock. Focus on being a business owner.*

When we consider how the stock market works, we must note that behind every stock is a business. Sometimes — often, in fact — a stock price will disconnect from the real value of a business, because that's the way the market works. So, if you own a fabulous business (whether a restaurant chain, or one superb restaurant, or a banquet hall, or a car dealership), who cares?

Well, if you decide that you wish to sell it, many care. Because you are now known as Mr. Willing Seller. And if I were sitting across the table, trying to buy it from you, I would be known as Mr. Willing Buyer.

And so we negotiate. Now, you, the seller, obviously have

one goal in mind. You would like to sell your business for the highest possible price.

My goal, as the buyer, is understandably to try to pay you the lowest possible price.

The price that we eventually agree upon will be known as The Fair Price — one you can live with and one I can live with. Of course, if your business is very good, I'm probably going to pay you a lot of money for it. (When Warren Buffett paid for Dairy Queen, and GEICO, and, in a multi-billion-dollar deal in late October 1999, MidAmerican Energy Holdings Company, he paid well for them, and negotiated for each one in its entirety.)

Of course, it was very difficult for me to get you to sell me your fine business at a ridiculously low price; in fact, it was impossible to do so. After all, you, as the owner of that chain of restaurants/banquet hall/car dealership, are in control. You either say "yes" or "no." If your business is that good, I'm probably going to have to pay you for the future earnings.

This wonderful business probably bought you your handsome house, educated your children, put quality clothes on your respective backs, allowed you to take lovely vacations. But I really don't care about all that. All I care about is future earnings!

I've done due diligence and I've checked out whether this is truly a quality business that will earn money in the future. So I'll come up with a price that will pay you for your future earnings, and one that will be fair to us both.

Let Us Learn to Love Volatility

When I buy shares of a business today on the stock markets of the world, in the depressed prices of 1999, I am able to buy a business at prices that I could never hope to negotiate from a "rational seller" across the table.

Here's a simple, very related example. In late 1998, Berkshire Hathaway was selling for over $81,000 a share. And at that towering price, Berkshire Hathaway *did not yet own* General Re — a $22-billion acquisition, the largest it ever made.

So what we have here is a phenomenal scenario. In November 1999, I could purchase shares of Berkshire Hathaway for nearly 30% less than what they were selling for at the end of 1998, just a year earlier, even though Berkshire Hathaway had since made the astounding addition of General Re, tens of billions more in assets than the company possessed when its price was some 30% higher. And I don't have to negotiate a new, higher price across the table. I can buy this amazing compounding machine on the stock market — a stock market that has utterly, irrationally discounted the value of Berkshire, based on nothing other than Rumour, Guesswork, and Stupidity (an off-key trio that tends to sing almost daily as background music to Dow Jones and Toronto Stock Exchange numbers).

Everything we do, as I've noted elsewhere in this book, is based on Crisis — producing Danger and Opportunity; remember those Chinese characters. Now, if the crisis is with Eaton's or Livent or Bre-X, you should certainly run like hell. Danger far outweighs anything.

But Coke merely stubbed its toe in 1999, and Gillette

caught a mild case of the flu. The world will continue to drink billions of glasses of Coke and continue to shave billions of day-old beards, and continue to visit the growing number of Disney theme parks — a new one is coming soon to China — and we all know this. Do we *really* want to be selling off our shares of Coke and Gillette and Disney — and Berkshire Hathaway — at the ridiculously low prices of 1999?

Ultimately, we contrarians would not be able to purchase shares of Coke and Gillette at these wonderfully low prices, were there not some *perceived* crisis driving down their stock prices. In other words, crisis is your friend. It gives you (and me, I can assure you) the chance to purchase chunks of these superb, long-lasting, universally recognized, internationally successful companies at very, very low prices. If it weren't for those (purported) crises of the late 1990s, you would have to pay $100 and more for each share of Coke and Gillette instead of the depressed prices of 1999.

The Opportunity today, at the beginning of the 21st century, is to buy at irrational (and irrationally low) prices. And if you do not have any free money to buy, simply ignore what has been (unfairly or stupidly) happening to the stocks of great companies like Coca-Cola, Gillette, and Berkshire Hathaway, and patiently wait for more rational, much higher, prices to return to those companies. (Companies that would cost far, far more to purchase, if you were negotiating from a private buyer, across a table.)

But because we are dealing with the stock market, where there are hundreds of thousands of owners and sellers, then you are able to negotiate these ridiculous, and often ridiculously low prices, based on (silly, irrational) stock market fluctuations. In his 1998 Berkshire Hathaway annual report, Warren Buffett asked his investors, "If you are a regular purchaser of hamburgers and you are not a cattle producer, do you want higher or lower beef prices?"

The key, clearly, is to understand how the stock market really works. And how it disconnects, from time to time, from real value. Remember how I pointed out that if you had a real business to sell, I would negotiate a fair price with you. You would push for the highest possible price, while I would try to get it for the lowest possible price. But eventually, if it's that good a business, I'd probably end up paying a large amount for it.

Some Further Thoughts about the Stock Market

Okay, now, let's look closer at your marvellous, wildly successful, worldwide chain of banquet halls, which is now publicly traded on a stock exchange. You've taken your company public, you've raised many millions of dollars, and you've opened this incredible business. You've got lots of partners now — pension funds, taxi drivers, lots of doctors, and hundreds of men and women who own shares in your firm.

Imagine, for the sake of the following discussion, that this company is still small and you haven't taken it public yet. Let's say that there are just 10 people who have put up $10,000 each, to buy a banquet hall for $100,000. The food is great, it's in a superb location, and there are tons of weddings, bar mitzvahs, and office parties.

But remember, there are just 10 owners at this stage of the business.

Here is the scenario. One of the 10 owners of this glorious

banquet hall runs into financial difficulty. Maybe his banker has called a loan, or he's being sued for divorce by his wife; perhaps he's been audited by the federal government and he owes tons of back taxes; that's not our concern. One of the owners of this hall is now in trouble, and needs some money badly — and soon.

Mr. I-Got-Money-Problems comes to the nine other partners in that great banquet hall — you and I are included — and he says to all of us, his voice shaking, "Guys, I'm in real trouble. I'll have to sell my share of the company. Could you pay me the $10,000 I put into it?"

None of us is that fond of this fellow, and we've known for weeks that he's in dire financial straits, so we all inform him, "Sorry, buddy, we don't want to buy your share for $10,000."

The poor guy goes away, and returns to the nine of us a few days later. "Listen, everyone. I'm truly desperate. I really do need to sell my shares. Will you buy them from me for $8000?"

And we, being the hard-nosed bargainers that we are, tell him, "Nope. We're not willing to pay that much for your shares. We're happy with the way things are, and have no desire to buy your portion."

He comes back a week later. "All right, you've got me against the wall. I'm going to offer all of you the buy of a lifetime. I'm prepared to sell my shares for $5000."

"Yes," we all agree. "We will indeed buy your shares for $5000."

Obviously, we remaining shareholders in this wonderful, successful banquet hall business are delighted. We've just managed to buy 10% of our company at a 50%-off sale. We have done good things — we've shrunk the number of share-holders from 10 to nine, meaning that the profits of this wonderful business will be divided among nine rather than 10. We got a fantastic price — a 50% discount on what we originally paid.

But what have else we just done? We have just slashed the value of this remarkable, money-making, immensely popular banquet hall company — dropping it precipitously from $100,000 down to $50,000.

Why? Because it's the last trade that sets the value of an entire company.

You can see what I'm getting at, I trust: *The real value of a business is not the silly, absurd, happenstance stock market price. The fact that it is publicly traded, and that there are willing buyers and willing sellers, and a market-maker in between — that is all that counts.* Remember, Benjamin Graham, Warren Buffett's mentor, described the stock market as "short term, a voting machine, but long term, a weighing machine."

Therein lies the stupidity, and the inefficiency, and irrationality, of the stock market. I think now of Mackenzie Financial Corporation, a superb mutual fund company, whose stock did not move for about four years in the early 1980s and was selling for a ridiculously low price — in spite of steady, constant growth of money-under-management and increasing management fees. I remember Michael Lee-Chin, the brilliant creator of the AIC funds, discussing this with me. "Richard," he said to me one day, "four years ago, Mackenzie was managing X number of dollars and bringing in X number of dollars in management fees. Today, it's managing many, many times that, yet its stock remains flat. If you owned 100% of this company and someone came to you today and said, 'I want to buy your entire firm for the same price that it was four years ago,' even though Mackenzie has grown its assets under administration and increased its management fees considerably and has no debt, and instead is piling up millions of dollars in cash on its balance sheet, would you sell the business to them at the same price that it was years earlier?"

We both agreed that the answer had to be "no!" And so, we were both able to keep the vast majority of our many clients invested in Mackenzie stock during that long, opportunistic period when the stock market was not reflecting Mackenzie's true value.

Here's another, related story. Wal-Mart stock peaked in 1994. There were "earnings disappointments" as profits fell from something like 26% to 17%. Brokers and mutual fund managers and the geniuses of Wall Street quickly decided that Wal-Mart was obviously no longer a fast-growing company. "Let's revise the price," they all agreed.

So, people who purchased Wal-Mart stock in 1994 found the value of their investment had dwindled by some 3% by the end of the following year. Their $100,000 was now worth $97,000. And it dropped another 3% each year through 1997, making the $100,000 worth more like $90,000.

But then, between 1997 and 1998, the stock doubled in price.

What happened? Well, for one thing, Wal-Mart came up to Canada in 1995 and opened 300 stores, and those stores soon became the most successful and largest retail organization in the country.

Now, imagine that you were Sam Walton, the inspired,

legendary owner of Wal-Mart, and it is now 1997. And someone approaches you and says, "Mr. Walton, I know that you own 100% of this company. I'd like to buy your entire firm at the same price it was back in 1994." (After all, the stock price remained flat, even a bit lower, over those three years.)

Some offer! Yet during those same years, you have opened 300 of the most successful, most profitable stores in the history of your firm, up in Canada, and hundreds more around the globe, and have pushed the Eaton's department store to the edge of bankruptcy.

If you were Sam Walton, you would probably thank me for this sparkling example of chutzpah and kick me out the door! The man who opened one store in a tiny, southern U.S. town, and then used the earnings and profits from that store to open two more, then five more, then 10 more? The man who eventually opened some 3500 stores around the world since the early 1960s and created a compounding machine not unlike that of Warren Buffett and Berkshire Hathaway? Why on earth would he sell his entire company at a discount merely because the stock exchanges and brokers and Wall Street mavens of the world decided that his company's shares were overpriced?

What a world this is! As I write these words as the new century begins, mutual funds sales are at record lows. Yet considering the thousands of bargains out there — in that so many quality companies have their shares at outrageously low prices — shouldn't mutual fund sales be at record highs?

I recall how, in 1991, AIC launched their now-famous Value Fund. They were happy to purchase shares of Berkshire Hathaway at $5600, instead of the $8900 they were selling for just a few days earlier. Michael Lee-Chin would have paid any price for Berkshire Hathaway, but since there was a *crisis* at the time, he was given the *opportunity* to buy shares at a one-third discount. Clearly, there wasn't much of a *danger*, was there, as Berkshire sells for over $60,000 a share at the turn of the century. But those who were dumping their shares at $5600 focused on danger while Mike saw only opportunity — and focused on a magnificent business.

Mutual funds are selling poorly, in late 1999, because people — like the stock markets they love to "play" and gamble in — are irrational. They will not become interested in investing again until mutual funds sales are booming again, and the prices of mutual funds (and the stocks they purchase) are at record highs once more. Only when they can join the crowd, and pay 10%, 20%, even 30% more for their mutual funds and stocks than they could have paid in mid-1999 — only then will they be happy. Only then will they feel secure.

What a world.

Berkshire Hathaway Provides Further Profound Insights

Let's look at Berkshire Hathaway again. In 1987, the company's stock on the New York Stock Exchange was selling at $4200 a share — not bad for a firm whose shares were $80 just a dozen years before.

Uh-oh! Later that same year, after the stock market crash of October, its price dropped to $2900. Oh no! But within two years, the stock had shot up to $8900. What a relief!

Oh dear, oh dear, oh dear: In 1991, when Saddam Hussein moved into Kuwait, Berkshire Hathaway shares dropped to

$5600! Panic ensued. "Sell!" cried your broker. "Get out while you can!" screamed your neighbour. "Let's cut our losses!" shouted your spouse.

But please remember. If you purchased Berkshire Hathaway shares in 1991 at $5600, you were actually voting. The one who sold his shares to you was voting with his feet — he thought the price could drop even more — while you were voting as well. But you were voting with your cheque-book. You knew full well that people would continue to drink Coke, and continue to shave with Gillette blades, and continue to read the *Washington Post* and *Newsweek*, and continue to buy furniture, and chocolates, and shoes, and . . .

What an advantage you had when you purchased Berkshire at $5600! Your fearful friend was dumping a stock, while you were purchasing a business (actually, several dozen superbly run businesses, which are no less well run when the stock is depressed than when the stock is at all-time highs).

Of course, if you had purchased those Berkshire Hathaway shares at $5600 each in 1991 and watched the shares zoom up to over $80,000 each in 1998, you are hardly crying in your beer (or in your Dairy Queen Blizzard, which Berkshire has owned for the past year, at nearly $1 billion dollars paid in cash); after all, even at the $60,000 range (that's what it's dancing at now, in late 1999), you haven't done too badly, have you?

An almost comical financial note, if it wasn't so shocking: In the last five trading days of October 1999 — during the same week of the 70th anniversary of the Great Stock Market Crash of late October 1929 — Berkshire Hathaway's stock price *rose* $9400. You read right. In merely five days, its stock price rose more in value than it was worth back in

1989, when it sold for $8900. And the stock shot up *another* $1600 the following Monday, the first day of November 1999.

So much for Berkshire's "terrifying" and "precipitous" collapse in 1999, when it "crumbled" from over $80,000 to around $55,000, and when a thousand business writers around the world wrote mockingly about "how the once-great Warren Buffett has met his Waterloo." Clearly, there are enough people out there who recognize that a few weak quarterly earning reports from Coca-Cola and Gillette do not stop people from reaching for a Diet Coke or trimming their whiskers. Why else would a stock shoot up nearly $10,000 — a nearly 20% increase of the stock price of Berkshire Hathaway — in five brief days of trading?

And as for those who own Berkshire Hathaway shares today, as the value hovers around $60,000 each, these investors might well hope that enough people will sell their shares, driving it down even more, so that they can buy more. He knows what those shares are really worth, and what astonishingly great companies Coke and Gillette and Walt Disney and Dairy Queen and General Re and MidAmerican Energy Holdings are.

Here is what is really ironic. When Berkshire Hathaway was selling at around $1000 a share back in the late 1970s, it did not own millions of shares of Coca-Cola and Gillette and American Express; it obviously did not own any MidAmerican Energy Holdings, purchased in late October 1999. No General Re. No GEICO. No Walt Disney. No . . .

Berkshire purchased its (often large, often 100%) portions of each of those amazing companies *after* it had reached $1000 a share.

I doubt if any of the handful of the original 100 owners of

Berkshire Hathaway (who purchased $100,000 each of the young, promising business at $80 a share) imagined in their wildest dreams that they would, one day, be part-owners of all of these wonderful, successful, profitable businesses. Not an inkling.

Berkshire Hathaway is a compounding machine. And as I noted at the close of an earlier chapter, even Albert Einstein believed that compounding was more powerful than splitting the atom.

Yes, stock market corrections can be gut wrenching; there's no other term for it. And to see your life savings drop from $100,000 to $50,000 (as those original 100 investors in Berkshire Hathaway experienced, back in the mid-'70s) is dreadful and terror-inducing.

Indeed, the owners of Berkshire stock in 1987 must have felt sick, seeing their $4200 shares drop to $2900 later the same year; the owners of Berkshire who paid $8900 in 1989 must have had many a sleepless night when each share dropped in value to $5600 less than two years later. But as I hope this chapter has shown — and that this entire book has proved to you — when Berkshire (and Coke, and TD Bank, and Mackenzie Financial Corporation, and Bombardier, and a hundred other magnificent companies) drops in stock price, *it does not drop in its inherent value and in its potential for future earnings.*

Indeed, an owner of a single Berkshire share in mid-October 1999, for which he paid $54,700, suddenly discovered in his morning newspaper that Warren Buffett had purchased a major energy company for over $2.2 billion *in cash* — making his business far more valuable than it had been minutes earlier!

And please recall how the market reacted. Berkshire's stock shot up nearly $10,000 in one week, to just under $64,000 — and the price of MidAmerican's shares zoomed up some 22% the same week, in what is fondly called "the halo effect." People recognized that, "if Warren Buffett bought this company, it must be deep discounted. It *must* be undervalued!" How fast the market can turn!

The one person (of the original 100) who stayed with Berkshire Hathaway, from $80 a share in 1973, down to $40, then up to $4200, then down to $2900, then up to $8900, then down to $5600, then up to over $80,000, then down to around $60,000 as I write these words — that one person owns over $70,000,000 in Berkshire stock in late 1999.

Why? Because he or she focused on Mr. Buffett's amazing *business*, and behaved like a *business owner*, while the other 99 original investors kept their eyes glued to the scoreboard, ignoring the playing field.

One more example. At the end of the 1900s, Toronto Dominion Bank was the exact same business as it had been only a few months before — probably even better. Yet its stock price was nearly 40% less at the end of 1999 than it had been early in 1999. That fact should certainly scream *buy!* and not *sell!* to the wise investor. But does it?

As you can see, without the "crisis," one never gets the opportunity. Yes, yes, crisis also produces "danger" — but is that danger real? Do Toronto Dominion, Coke, Gillette, Berkshire Hathaway, and hundreds of other magnificent businesses have fatal diseases (as of late 1999), or have they merely stubbed their respective toes?

I think you know the answer to that.

Postscript: In the first few days of November 1999 an article ran in the *Globe and Mail* about one of the giants of the computer industry, Michael Dell. It noted that Mr. Dell's stock had gone up 71,000% since its inception.

Would you care to guess how many enjoyed those billions of dollars of increase? Michael Dell, of course. A tiny handful of associates, perhaps. Who else?

Pity poor Michael Dell. He had no time to watch his stock price rise and fall and rise and rise and rise. He was too busy running and building a great business. On the other hand, most of the other original investors turned into speculators, focusing on the stock price. They allowed themselves to be talked out of Dell, and took their early profits — profits that could have been thousands of times greater had they only focused on what was a superb company.

Which is why Michael Dell is a multi-billionaire, as is Warren Buffett.

Of course, armed with the above facts, you are now ready to become a billionaire yourself.

Or at least to invest like one.

17

Seek Out a Full-Service
Financial Advisor

I N choosing an investment advisor, you need to find someone who has a very profound philosophy about how money
should be managed. I firmly believe that the success of any
investment will come from two primary sources: the quality
of investment made on behalf of the investor (whether it be
mutual funds or in a single business, through the purchase of
common stock), and the duration of time that it is held.

I have often mentioned in these pages the awesome story
of Coca-Cola; that a $40 investment made in 1919 was worth
well over $5 million in late 1999. It is clear from that single
company's history that the root of all wealth lies in ownership of an excellent business, and the indefinite time period
it is owned.

I must be vulgar here, for emphasis. Most financial portfolios are structured for mediocrity, since the majority of
investment advisors are simply protecting their asses. And

if they are recommending mutual funds, then the managers of those funds are also protecting their own asses.

In the case of most brokers, if you say that you wish to put $100,000 into a portfolio of stocks, most will recommend between five and 10 companies. The average mutual funds salesperson will recommend a half dozen mutual funds — and each one of them has dozens of stocks in its possession. So you end up owning many hundreds of stocks, which only guarantees that your portfolio will be far too over-diversified to bring in any good returns. This over-diversification only guarantees mediocrity, while not even guaranteeing that you will have no loss of principal.

If your investment advisor has no real philosophy, he will sell you what Warren Buffett calls "the Noah style of investment" — two of these, two of those, two of them, and so on. This occurs because there is no serious belief in anything.

Real growth, as I keep noting, is generated by investing in a few solid investments, not dozens or hundreds. Mr. Buffett made another good comment on this question worth noting: that in a lifetime of investing, if you were given only 20 good ideas, and if every time you used one of them you had to punch a card (leaving 19, then 18, and so on), you would be a lot more careful and thoughtful about how to allocate your investment capital. This is because you would know that you had only a limited amount of opportunity in your lifetime and would therefore be a lot less reluctant to simply blunder along. This is a good attitude.

So where does the "cover your ass" problem arise? It is always present when you have mutual funds managers who have no incentive to do anything special for their investors, because they want to keep their jobs. In 1996, a prominent manager of a major mutual fund company in the United States decided to do something "special." He suddenly withdrew most of the tens of millions his fund had invested in stocks and placed it heavily into bonds. The value of the bonds went down while stocks prices shot up, leading to mediocre returns for a mutual fund that had been a stellar performer to that point. He was unceremoniously fired.

In brief, everyone is covering his or her respective ass by over-diversifying, or by going with the latest, "special" trend or fad.

A further dilemma arises when investment advisors try to sell mutual funds by their past performance. ("Look! The XYZ fund shot up 28% last year. It's got a great track record.") Now, with a quality stock of a great company such as a Coca-Cola or a Microsoft or a major bank, there could well be some truth in that suggestion. But when talking about mutual funds, there is hardly any relevance to such a statement.

Why? Well, I know one very major mutual fund that bought and sold some 600 different common stocks during 1995. Indeed, many mutual funds don't have the same stocks in their portfolios only two weeks after they buy them. So how can any mutual fund dealer try to sell a particular fund on its past performance only, when the contents of that fund are very often greatly changed?

As I've noted often throughout this book, all wealth is created by taking intelligent risk. But if you believe that you can avoid risk by buying bonds, you are sadly mistaken. Bonds, please remember, have a minimum floor, all right, but they also have a maximum ceiling. With the ownership of a good business (through the purchase of its common stock), however, there is neither a floor nor a ceiling. True, that lack of a floor in terms of its value can be off-putting to many. But with a magnificent stock like, say, Gillette, that floor is never too low, whereas its ceiling can rise forever.

Here's an ugly bond story, and it has to do with a company whose products we have all loved since our youth. Walt Disney did a horrible thing to a group of bondholders a few years ago when it borrowed $50 million to make the animated motion picture *The Lion King*.

The eventual profits, as you may be aware, from sale of movie tickets, books, the video, plush toys, and countless other merchandising spinoffs, had already surpassed, by early 1997, $1 billion (yes, one thousand million dollars), and counting.

So what was the terrible thing that this grand company did to those bondholders? It merely paid them back their $50 million, plus a small interest on the loan.

They received no free movie passes. They obtained no free T-shirts — nor any profit on the hundreds of thousands sold. They got no free CD of the great soundtrack. They were handed no complimentary videos for their kids. Nor were they invited to the annual meeting of the company.

The holders of those bonds received nothing but an insultingly small interest on their loan, because bondholders own nothing. True, there was no floor on their investment, so they could never "lose it all." But there was a very claustrophobic ceiling. So while they made their 6, 7, or 8 percent on their loan to Walt Disney, those who had been wise enough to purchase common shares in the company more than doubled their money over the same period. Not too smart. But then, the enormous, stunning profits of *The Lion King* belonged only to shareholders of Walt Disney stock, and nobody else.

As you can see, choosing a good investment advisor is not easy. But it's a lot less difficult when you know to look for one with a solid philosophy of investment, a philosophy that argues that stocks are parts of businesses; that the advisor wants to create value for you by helping you to own those businesses for generations — not till just next week or next month or even next year.

Here's the real catch. You must find an investment advisor who will help you do the things that you should do — not the things that you want to do. Let me explain. The natural tendencies of the vast majority of us are usually antagonistic to wealth creation, whether due to our desire to Get Rich Quick or to Take the Profits and Run. So what we want to do and what we should do are not necessarily the same.

Think about it. Over the past 70 years, the Dow Jones Industrial Average has risen from 40 to over 11,000. More wealth has been created for a generation of North Americans than any time in history, yet most of that money came into the market only over the past three years. (Those high interest rates, which have been declining steadily over the past two decades, pauperized a generation who were fearful of investing; they were thrilled to get 12% or more at their neighbourhood banks.) So most people are suicidal with their own, macho tendencies towards investment — invariably, they want to buy high and sell low, often without even knowing it.

I can assure you of several constants. Declines in the market and in stock prices are a certainty, all right — but they are invariably temporary. It is the advances that are permanent; they are the only things that truly last. Over the long term, the stock market will deliver superior returns.

The job of the good investment advisor, then, is to help you enjoy every day of those wonderful, marvellous advances in the stock market. There's a price tag, of course, and that is that you must stay with all the declines, as well as with the advances. But I swear to you, this is not too high a price to pay.

Of course, it takes courage to hold your course. Markets are cyclical and can be unpredictable, even absurd. There are those inevitable corrections, which scare the hell out of 90% of people, who panic and sell their shares — leaving wise men and women like you to look at this (brief) bear market and see a flashing neon sign that reads THE BIG SALE IS ON. BUY NOW! Which is when you should be buying even more common shares of fine businesses than ever.

You need an investment advisor who will help you put together an investment program, and then keep it together, against your natural, self-destructive tendencies. Because if you leave the market during its (inevitable) declines, you will miss the opportunities for those inevitable market rises. And then, if the market rises when you are out of it, you might not want to get back in again.

So you have to stay invested. Find an investment advisor who will help you to "turn off" the stock market and its scoreboard and focus instead on the playing field. To help you realize that even if we are in an economic slump, or the province of Quebec is threatening separation, or there are riots on the streets of American cities, or war in the Balkans, these have nothing to do with your being a part-owner of some of the world's great businesses — businesses that will continue to produce great earnings over time.

Your investment advisor should really be more of a coach,

someone who has your well-being and your best interests at heart. And these interests should include everything from wealth creation to multi-generational wealth creation, especially estate planning, wills, transferring assets to the second generation, making sure that you can take care of your parents in the best possible fashion, educate your grandchildren, and much more.

You don't necessarily want an investment advisor to educate you; you have done that by reading this book. You need one who will have the trust and faith to help you keep investing in, and holding, great common stock. To help you keep your fears at bay. To agree with you that the market is not an end in itself, but a means to an end — to achieve your financial goals and dreams, and those of your descendants. (And don't forget what I've noted earlier. Thirty years ago, when someone retired, that person could expect only another eight years of life; today, a retiree can look forward to another quarter century on this earth. All the more time to see great stocks increase in value; all the more time that you will need successful investments to pay your bills.)

The quality investment advisor should be concerned with all of these things, not merely angling to pick up a commission cheque. Which is why the financial advisor you eventually choose to work with should have a profound, sincere, steady, proven investment philosophy — like the one I have been espousing throughout this book.

Investing the Billionaire's Way. My title says it all.

Conclusion

Imagine that in some private business you own a small share that cost you $1000. One of your partners, named Mr. Market, is very obliging indeed. Every day he tells you what he thinks your interest is worth and, furthermore, offers either to buy you out or sell you an additional interest on that basis. Sometimes his idea of value appears plausible; often, on the other hand, Mr. Market lets his enthusiasm or his fears run away with him, and the value he proposes seems to you a little short of silly.

BENJAMIN GRAHAM, in the 1950s

I am not in the business of predicting general stock market or business fluctuations. If you think I can do this, or think it is essential to an investment program, you should not be in the partnership.

WARREN BUFFETT, early in his partnership, in the 1950s

Now, who could argue with the great Benjamin Graham, and his renowned disciple, Warren Buffett? I hope that this book has convinced you that there is simply no alternative to investing in order to build a nest egg. As I've noted above, there are only three things one can do with money: Lend it, spend it, or invest in something that has the potential to increase in value over time. In every corner of the Free World (and more and more, in places like China and Cuba as well, for the passion for capitalism is universal), wealth has always been created through business ownership — with the goal of every business being to make money for its shareholders, through providing goods and services to a consumer base.

One might joke that there are some alternatives to investing in a business — or, through the purchase of its common stock, in small parts of a business. After all, you can always marry a wealthy man or woman. Or you can choose to be born into (or be adopted by) a rich family. But these seem a bit less likely and more difficult than investing in the shares of a good company.

There is a phrase I often quote in my seminars: "Whatsoever I believe will come to pass in my life; therefore, what I must believe, I must expect. And what I expect, I must experience."

A person who is poor sometimes has a poor attitude and lacks the courage and moral fibre to do what is right. And what is right is to invest wisely and for long periods of time. Men and women who do not invest, who save their money in bank accounts or in GICs or U.S. or Canada Savings Bonds, who don't leave mediocre jobs to start their own businesses and follow their dreams — these people fail to act thoughtfully, because they fear failure. And, sadly, that fear will attract the very things they fear the most: poverty, despair, and a retirement that will be hungry and even frightening.

Do recall what I wrote, many chapters ago, near the start of this book: We are all the custodians to the 60- or 70-year-old man or woman we shall be some day. And if we were to meet our future selves on the road, and those people asked us why there was no money, we would want to be able to avoid the terribly common reply: "I worked all my life, I raised a family, I saved money — but I didn't invest, because I feared that I might lose money." That sort of existence always ends up poor.

My conclusion, then, is really the theme of this entire book: Unless you invest, you will be poor. Unless you invest, you will never be able to move from fear to infinity. So invest, and invest wisely, and you will grow rich.

The choice is up to you.

One Woman's
Astonishing Story

M ANY readers may have noticed in their daily newspapers a few years ago — the story was picked up across
North America — a touching tale of a lonely old woman who
left many millions of dollars after she died to a university she
never attended, "so women would be better treated than I
had been in my career."

It was with great pleasure that I came across a reprint of
a fine article about this extraordinary woman, Anne Scheiber,
in the April 1997 issue of *Reader's Digest*, which first
appeared in the *Washington Post* on December 17, 1995. I
have requested and received permission to reproduce this
story, written by James K. Glassman, since it captures
exquisitely what I have been sharing with you throughout
this book.

Here is the article, reprinted in full, which I feel makes a
perfect appendix to this book; my thanks to journalist

Glassman for finding the moral to this story, beyond the simple facts of the woman's generosity in her will.

How to Build a Big Nest Egg

When the story came out in the newspapers two years ago [1993], it seemed too good to be true. A little old lady, living alone in a run-down studio apartment, parlays $5,000 out of her savings into a $20-million fortune and leaves almost all of it to a university that had never heard of her. Even better, she has the last laugh on her ex-employer, an outfit that she felt denied her promotions because she was a woman.

But it was all true. The heroine, Anne Scheiber, worked for the U.S. Internal Revenue Service. Despite her law degree, the IRS never promoted her or paid her more than $3,150 a year ($28,000 in today's money). She retired in 1943 and put her money in stocks. Last year Yeshiva University in New York City found that it was the beneficiary of her estate.

The best part of this story is that by following her investment guidelines, you can do almost as well as this little old lady did. Here are the lessons of Anne Scheiber's amazing success:

Start early. Scheiber was 51 when she invested her $5,000 and 101 when she died. Her companies earned profits on their profits over and over, and in the long run, share prices grew along with corporate earnings, as they almost always do.

Stocks need many years for this "miracle of compounding" to work. That's why the single most important factor in stock-market success is time.

If you want to emulate Scheiber, you should begin much earlier — in your 20s or 30s. At an annual growth rate of 12 percent, an investment of $1,000 in stocks today will become about $100,000 in the year 2036. Assume inflation at three to four percent annually, and that $100,000 will be worth about $25,500 in today's dollars. Not bad.

Buy stocks. As an IRS auditor dealing with estates, Scheiber noticed that the very rich tended to own common stock. This was no fluke. Since 1926 the average annual return on stocks in the United States has been 12.2 percent, compared with 5.7 percent for corporate bonds and 3.7 percent for short-term Treasury bills.

If Scheiber had invested only in bonds, her $5,000 would have grown to only about $80,000.

In the late 1970s, Scheiber's stockbroker, William Fay of Merrill Lynch & Co., did persuade her to use some of her stock dividends to buy municipal bonds — a sensible move for a woman in her 80s since, in the short term, bonds are less risky than stocks. But this move into bonds probably limited the total value of her portfolio.

Buy and hold. "She just held on to what she bought and rarely sold anything," says Fay of his client. "She believed in these companies. She just stayed with them. She did not care if the market was up or down."

Scheiber's success is dramatic proof of how well a simple buy-and-hold strategy works. In 1953 she bought 500 shares of Schering-Plough Corp., the pharmaceutical company, for about $6,000. And she just held on. Today, through stock splits, those original 500 shares have become 64,000 shares, worth $3.64 million.

Another of her longtime holdings, Coca-Cola Co., increased in value from $28,000 to $720,000 in 15 years. That doesn't even include $62,000 in dividends.

All of her stocks went through rough patches. Fay says there was a time "during the '70s when Schering-Plough lost half its value." But Scheiber didn't sell, and she was amply awarded for her discipline.

Minimize taxes. Scheiber denied the IRS estate taxes at her death by leaving her money to a nonprofit institution. More important, though, she generally avoided capital-gains taxes during her life.

It's a pleasant quirk of the U.S. [and Canadian] tax code that taxes on profits aren't owed until you sell an asset.

If you can hold stocks until your retirement, you've created what amounts to an unlimited individual retirement account [IRA — the equivalent of Canada's RRSP]. Non-IRA investors who churn their portfolios, on the other hand, incur not only brokerage commissions but also repeated tax bites that drastically reduce the power of compounding.

Buy quality. Scheiber avoided fads. She bought solid companies with good balance sheets and strong reputations rather than trying to find the next Microsoft in its cradle. "She focused on franchise names," says Fay. Among them: PepsiCo, Exxon, Chrysler, Warner-Lambert.

Scheiber also bought what she knew. "She was drawn to these stocks by their products," Fay says. She understood pharmaceuticals, so she bought Pfizer, Bristol-Myers and Schering-Plough. She loved the movies, so she bought Loews, which owned a chain of theatres. "She had faith in these companies," according to Fay.

Never touch capital. This is the famous admonition of old wealth, and Scheiber followed it to the hilt. She left her Merrill Lynch account alone and reinvested all the dividends and interest.

"She had the mentality," says Fay, "that she had to exist on her small IRS pension and Social Security." But Scheiber went to extremes. "She had few friends," Fay points out. "By our standards she was an unhappy person, totally consumed by her securities accounts and her money." Making millions doesn't require this kind of obsession. Start early, and you may end up like Anne Scheiber — only a lot happier.